FACE-LIFT APARTHEID

South Africa after Soweto

by

Judy Seidman

INTERNATIONAL DEFENSE & AID FUND
for Southern Africa
P. O. BOX 17
CAMBRIDGE, MA. 02138

International Defence and Aid Fund
for Southern Africa

London 1980

The International Defence and Aid Fund for Southern Africa has the following objects:—

1. To aid, defend and rehabilitate the victims of unjust legislation and oppressive and arbitrary procedures;

2. To support their families and dependants;

3. To keep the conscience of the world alive to the issues at stake.

ISBN No. 0 904759 39 3

Contents

Introduction

Time is running out—time has run out ... I don't think
we have five years to play with.
                    Rear Admiral Edwards, South African Defence Force,
                                                    February 1978[1]

This pessimistic statement was made two years after Soweto. The black
townships erupted in 1976: across the country students attacked the government
with whatever came to hand, stones and fire against a modern arsenal ranging
from tear-gas machines to guns and helicopters. The government answered with
widespread shootings. By December 1976, 499 Africans were listed as dead from
gunshots in funeral parlours and police and hospital records; unofficial estimates
of the number of dead rose as high as 5,000.[2] Yet the protests continued sporadi-
cally until 1978, Soweto followed by Cape Town followed by East London and
Port Elizabeth. Even such remote places as Sibasa, "capital" of the Venda
bantustan, faced student uprisings.

In some ways, the townships never returned to pre-1976 normal. The school
boycott that triggered the demonstrations halted in early 1979, but secondary
schools in Soweto never fully regained their previous enrolment. Everyday
police patrols in townships, as opposed to massive semi-military "crime prevention sweeps", are practically non-existent with the result that, despite stringently
enforced hours limiting petrol sales in white South Africa, petrol is available
within the townships all night and all weekend, because garage owners do not
fear police visits. According to the Security Police, an estimated four thousand
Africans have fled South Africa for guerilla training camps to the north, and
thousands more are still leaving.[3]

Internationally, the white government's position in 1978 appeared equally
precarious. The collapse of Portuguese colonialism in 1974 first breached the
cordon sanitaire of white states isolating South Africa from independent Africa.
Mozambique and Angola no longer acted as buffers against freedom movements;
instead, they provided bases for guerillas operating in Namibia, Zimbabwe and
ultimately South Africa. Namibia and Zimbabwe themselves had become
involved in guerilla wars, causing a continual drain on South Africa's economic
and military strength. Above all hovered the danger that one of these guerilla
movements would soon govern Namibia or Zimbabwe (as indeed happened) and
in turn provide bases for direct attacks upon South Africa.

Further, white South Africa was shocked to discover that they could not depend upon Western support automatically, even if the menace was labelled "communist". In 1975 South African troops invaded Angola in an attempt to destroy the as yet shaky control of the MPLA; the MPLA received aid from Cuban troops to force back the South African army. South Africa claimed it had been promised large-scale American military support which failed to materialize. Instead, the Western powers have had more and more trouble avoiding United Nations' calls for sanctions against South Africa. In November 1977 the United Nations imposed a mandatory arms embargo on South Africa.

By 1978, then, the white South African government occupied an increasingly dangerous position. On the one hand, there was an explosive (if temporarily quiescent) black majority upon whose labour South Africa depends; on the other, an increasingly hostile international front. The apartheid state had to find a formula to diffuse these threats without destroying its own economic and political foundations. This book examines the formula which has been found, looking at the changes the government has made in apartheid, and their impact upon the structure of South African society.

Apartheid: how the system works

The population of South Africa is one-fifth white and four-fifths black. The white minority controls the political and economic structure; the black majority provides cheap labour within this white-controlled arena. This dichotomy was deliberately created and maintained. The first laws depriving Africans of legal rights to the land were passed in the nineteenth century. By 1940 there was a whole battery of laws restricting Africans' rights to own land, to travel, to work in skilled jobs, to vote, to organize, and so on. Then in the 1950s the Nationalist government systematically reworked these laws into one comprehensive structure, known as *Apartheid* (literally, "separateness").

The keystone of apartheid is the Bantustan (officially Homelands or Black States) policy. The African population is relegated to areas amounting to 13% of the land, previously known as "native reserves", often the poorest and least productive parts, scattered in small sections on the fringes of the industrialized heart of South Africa. To these lands, now labelled "tribal homelands", all Africans belong it is claimed; the rest of the country belongs to the whites.[4]

Blacks are only allowed to live on the "white land"—the other 87%—if they are economically productive. The unemployed, the old, and the very young, are to be sent away to the "homelands".

To enforce this, the government has strengthened the rigid system of control over the population's movements, known as the pass laws. Every African over the age of 16 has to carry a pass, a small book containing the holder's official life. The pass shows where the holder is permitted to live, and in what job he or she is permitted to work; whether he or she is in school or has permission to seek work; whether he or she is allowed to travel to a particular place.

Africans are particularly restricted from living in urban areas. The government calls this "influx control". The main influx control law, Section 10 (1) of the Bantu (Urban Areas) Consolidation Act, allows an African to live in an urban area only if he has since birth continuously lived in that area (Section 10 (1) (a)), or if he has held the same job in that area for at least ten years (Section 10 (1) (b)); if he or she is the wife or dependent child of someone who qualifies under the above two rules (Section 10 (1) (c)), or if he or she is employed on contract in the urban area, his or her "permanent" residence then being in a "homeland" (Section 10 (1) (d)). Anyone found illegally in an urban area is liable under these laws to be "endorsed out"—"deported" to his "homeland". In 1977 a quarter of a million Africans suffered arrest for pass and influx control violations.[5]

In these ways much of the African workforce has been forced into migrant labour. Their families and "homes" remain in or have been removed to the bantustans. The worker must leave his family for most of the year to work in a white area on contract. Such black workers live in single-sex hostels and compounds. The family in the "homeland" survives on whatever money the breadwinner sends back to them; this money is eked out often by a small vegetable plot and a few animals, but many families have neither the labour nor the land nor the resources to make farming a reliable income.

This control on movement is backed up by political control. Africans have no say in the national government. They cannot vote in national elections. They are allowed to vote for their "homeland governments" under controlled conditions, thereby allowing them an illusion of influence over a fragmented thirteen per cent of the land and its products. Just how meaningful this is can be illustrated by the fact that the Transkei, the most coherent in land area and longest "independent" of the bantustans, had to be subsidized by the South African government in 1978 to the tune of R113 million, or 75% of its total budget.[6]

Black opportunities are further hampered by an educational structure that ensured that "natives will be taught from childhood to realize that equality with Europeans is not for them".[7] The curriculum is distorted, preventing pupils from gaining much knowledge of the world outside the apartheid system. The physical conditions are crippling, with over-crowded classrooms, few textbooks, badly trained teachers. In 1975-76 the government allocated 2.88% of the budget for white education, 0.53% for Coloured, 0.22% for Asian, and 0.70% for African education.[8]

Lastly, apartheid rests upon rigid security legislation. The South African authorities can arrest anyone upon suspicion and hold them effectively indefinitely; they can "ban" a person, making it illegal for that person to participate in any political activities or even talk to more than one other person at one time; they have control over what information can be distributed and read; they have a police force notorious for torture and death in detention.

The apartheid structure enables most of the white population to live like those with high incomes in America or Britain. They own cars and swimming pools and television sets and freezers. Their children are highly educated, at state expense, and their health services although not free are quite possibly the best in the world. High wages for whites are usual.

The average black South African wage-earner—for those who are employed—earns a quarter of the average American wage, a third of the average British wage. The South African Department of Statistics claimed in 1978 that the average African wage was R120 per month, compared to R536 per month for whites.[9] The minimal living level, the lowest level of income upon which it is calculated a family of four should be able to survive, was in July 1978 in Soweto about R160 per month.[10] One survey showed that, even with more than one wage earner per household, just under half of the households surveyed (in Johannesburg, Pretoria, Durban, Port Elizabeth and Bloemfontein) earned incomes below the minimum level needed to survive.[11] Blacks are forced to live in townships outside the cities, without indoor sanitation, electricity, or paved roads. Families are forced to split up by the migrant labour system. Education is hard to come by, and by law the content is very limited.

But apartheid hits worst those who are "removed" from the cities to the bantustans. These people are dumped on the land, without resources, sometimes with only tents as shelter, sometimes in "resettlement camps" without adequate food or water. Policy determines that these people are the economically unproductive, so they tend to be the old, mothers and children, the sick. Much of the land set aside for the "homelands" is poor, but even where it is potentially productive it is too drastically overcrowded to enable people to live off it. As a result, the bantustan population lives on the brink of starvation:

"These people are hungry", an agricultural training officer in the Msinga district of Zululand claims. "There are people here who by all normal standards should be dead. They are alive only because their neighbours help them, in the knowledge that they might find themselves in a similar plight the next day".[12]

Thornhill Resettlement Camp, in the Ciskei, became notorious in January 1977 when a doctor revealed a large number of deaths from malnutrition among the 10,000 inhabitants, reporting that:

"The babies are dying of gastro-enteritis and diarrhoea . . . the adult deaths are attributable to malnutrition and consequent incidence of diseases like kwashiorkor, tuberculosis and pellagra".[13]

The government, under pressure, sent emergency rations; the doctor was transferred. A year later, Thornhill again made news with a typhoid epidemic: three died and 130 cases were treated, according to official statistics. Apparently the emergency rations rushed in after the first scandal were of a lower standard than those supplied to Boer War concentration camp internees; and in any case the rations were discontinued after popular interest waned.[14]

This case is unusual in that it was published. The evidence indicates these conditions are not that uncommon among people who have been resettled. Nationwide child mortality rates for the African population have not been published since 1963, when 300 to 400 out of a thousand children born died before they were four (for whites the figure was 27 out of a thousand births.)[15] But one recent study suggests that in rural areas "infant mortality among African children was 25 times that of white children, i.e. 530 per 1,000 . . . 50 to 60 % of them die before the age of 5". This study concludes that infant mortality for Africans has actually risen since the 1960s.[16]

The South African government has encouraged (some say "forced") these bantustans to become "independent" nations, electing their own governments. The territories are too physically fragmented, too poor and too overcrowded to ever be more than nominally independent. Yet the South African government, having granted this "independence", claims it has no responsibility for the people in the bantustans; any economic aid it may give to them counts as pure philanthropy. Moreover, under the bantustan programme all Africans are to become "citizens" of independent "Black States", thereby losing any claim to political and civil rights in the rest of South Africa.

This then constituted the apartheid system of the mid-1970s. It is primarily a system of exploitation based on a division of society in terms of race. The simple segregation of restaurants and restrooms (so-called "petty apartheid") carried the logic of this division into everyday life, and made everyday life just that much more miserable for the Africans. But apartheid theorists always intended petty apartheid to be a temporary measure, to enforce racial separation until the Grand Apartheid plans made integration out of the question.[17] The heart of the apartheid system (grand apartheid) lies in influx control, passes, resettlement and migrant labour.

The events of the mid-1970s threatened this system. However, the Nationalist Party had created this structure over the previous twenty years: it remained determined to save it despite internal revolt and international disapproval.

The "Save South Africa" Formula

The government therefore looked for some solution to the threats to apartheid. The simplest response lay with the military. The Defence budget of April 1979 reached a new level (nearly double the 1975 budget) of R1,857,000,000.[18] White males face a military draft that is extended for longer and longer periods as the military presence grows in the border areas in Namibia. And in October 1979 the US government reluctantly admitted that they held some evidence of a South African nuclear explosion.

But military strength, as the world has recognised since Vietnam, does not necessarily defeat a guerilla movement which has popular backing. Within the South African government pressure built up for some kind of change that would gain the support of at least a part of the black population for the existing structure. This is the key to the recent changes: they aim to preserve the existing structure, not destroy it.

The solution the government decided upon entailed building up a group of Africans with some stake in the existing system, described, not entirely correctly, as a "black middle class". Apartheid has hitherto blocked the formation of such a group. By law, Africans could not work in skilled jobs, could only own some types of businesses, could not employ whites, and so on. Further, even if they made some money, Africans were limited in what they could buy with it. They could not own a house or property in urban areas, they could not get a good education in South Africa, they could not even eat in the best restaurants. The new government policy is aimed at enabling a small number of Africans to prosper; this group would then have reason to ally themselves with the white government against the aspirations of the black majority. As Patrick Laurence, the *Rand Daily Mail*'s political correspondent summarized in December 1978:

> The strategy was to woo the black middle class as an ally of the white minority, or, as an Afrikaans newspaper put it, to consolidate the middle class as a bastion against attack on South Africa's free capitalist way of life. The Nationalist Party appropriated the liberal strategy of alliance with the black bourgeiosie and grafted it on to its earlier policy of winning over the chiefs and headmen through the homelands policy . . .

> The success or failure of the policy is of crucial importance to the future of South Africa. On it will depend the extent to which the authorities can win black allies and on that, in turn, will determine in what measure the insurgents are isolated.[19]

But if on the one hand a small group is to be built up into a black elite, on the other hand the majority of Africans must be forced even more rigorously into the apartheid pattern. The *Financial Mail* pinpointed the dichotomy neatly: "Government's aim of course, is to build up a stable black urban middle class *to the exclusion* of migrants and homelanders"[20] (*emphasis added*).

This internal policy has been accompanied by a new South African political offensive (to parallel its military offensive) to regain its former domination of the Southern African region. However, the new "constellation of states" which South Africa hopes to form, based on "common interests and developing mutual relations", will only sound credible if South Africa makes some attempts to placate its own African population.

The first steps towards the new internal policy were taken by the Vorster government. However, it is only since the ascent of Mr. P. W. Botha as Prime Minister that it has been applied explicitly:

> Having correctly assessed the seriousness and urgency of both the international and domestic situations, Botha has made it clear that, regardless of political losses and a right wing backlash, he is determined to implement these changes regarded as vital to South Africa's survival.[21]

The Botha government does not differ fundamentally from its predecessors on the question of grand apartheid, despite the new government's image:

> It might be argued that the *verligtes* ("enlightened" Afrikaner Nationalists) have been developing a more sophisticated form of apartheid, secure in their

belief that allowing it to become a little frayed round the edges will not in any way undermine the core of their policies.[22]

The big difference is that Mr. P. W. Botha seemed willing, if necessary, to split the traditional Afrikaner alliances in order to win the support of "Big Business", to a large extent English-speaking with international connections. The Vorster approach—as revealed at length in the Information Department scandal—was to buy foreign opinion (literally, in the case of the *Washington Star*) by underhand measures. Mr. P. W. Botha in contrast hopes to win the international support that apartheid so disastrously lacks by his new policy; according to Patrick Laurence, the new strategy

. . . has two recommendations: it creates a buffer between the white elite and the relatively impoverished black masses, and thereby transfers a racial struggle between white and black into an ideological one between capitalism and Marxism.[23]

Those who eagerly anticipate these announced changes, on viewing the product of government deliberations (as opposed to the press releases), on occasion asked whether the government ever planned to introduce the changes in good faith. The London *Times* commented:

It is all very well for Mr. Botha's Minister for Cooperation and Development, Dr. Piet Koornhof, to declare that "apartheid is dead". But as Desmond Tutu, the secretary-general of the South African Council of Churches remarked, they "want to see the corpse first".[24]

Such doubts, perhaps, cannot be resolved at least for the present. But some idea of the pressures involved can be developed by looking at the forces for and against change within the government itself.

The forces for and against change

"Big Business" and especially the trans-national corporations operating within South Africa, want more rapid change. As Mr. Harry Oppenheimer, chief of Anglo-American Corporation, South Africa's largest corporation, said in 1976:

In particular, those of us who believe that private enterprise is the system best calculated to widen the areas of individual choice—to open up new opportunities and raise the standard of life—have to show very clearly that this private enterprise system is not something which bears the label "for whites only". In South Africa we need, for our security and for our development, a real unity in the country to resist events such as we have seen taking place in Angola, but it is surely intensely illogical to ask a lot of black people to stand together with whites in order to oppose Communist aggression if, at the same time, by law and custom, they are excluded from most of the benefits which are conferred by the free enterprise system."[25]

Apartheid has provided the mines and factories of free enterprise with cheap labour, which business had no hesitation in exploiting, using labour-intensive methods instead of machines. Indeed the average profit returns on investments

11

in South Africa from 1960–1970 were 18.6%, compared to 11% for the rest of the world.[26]

These methods however have become more of a liability than an advantage now. Trans-national corporations are coming under attack in the mother countries and the rest of the world for investment in a racist system. And the cheap labour system itself has begun to look insecure. South Africa has always depended upon its neighbouring countries for a supply of migrant labour, especially for the crucial but dangerous, ill-paid and uncomfortable jobs in the mines. In 1970, 44% of South Africa's black miners came from Mozambique and other "tropical areas" (Angola and Malawi in particular). Another 21% came from Botswana, Lesotho and Swaziland. By the mid-1970s, with socialist-orientated governments in Angola and Mozambique, war in Zimbabwe and Namibia and political conflict on her own borders, and finally a boycott of migrant labour by Malawi, South Africa could not rely upon this supply of migrant labour any more. In fact, Mozambique has not yet officially tried to cut off South Africa's migrant labour supply, but nonetheless, in 1976 Mozambique's migrant labour had dropped to slightly over one-third of its previous supply, and although the number slightly increased in 1977, it decreased again in 1978. By 1977, the migrants from Mozambique and the "tropical areas" made up a bare 14% of the total percentage of black miners. The mines to date have replaced these with men from within South Africa: thus the number of miners from the Cape went up by 2½ times, from the Orange Free State by four times, and so on for the bantustans in all the provinces in the same period (1970–77).[27]

But the bantustans cannot be counted upon as an endless supply of labour at sub-subsistence wage levels and low skills, especially since the 1976 uprising showed that South Africa's black population would not remain quiet forever. Indeed, industry was already pressing for more capital-intensive techniques before the Soweto events. Harry Oppenheimer, head of Anglo-American, told the London Stock Exchange on 18 May 1976:

The increase in black wages (*in the five years before 1976*) reflects the beginning of a process, still actively continuing, of a change-over from a labour-intensive, low-wage, low-productivity economic system—typical of industrial development in its earliest stages—to the capital-intensive, high-wage high-productivity system which characterizes the advanced industrialized countries.

He went on to emphasize that:

. . . the migrant labour system becomes less and less appropriate from an economic point of view as well as, of course, from a social and moral point of view. This does not mean, unfortunately, that it is to foresee a time when migrant labour, particularly in the gold mining industry, can be completely phased out . . .[28]

Big business has pushed for a higher level of mechanization. The white elite, however, is not large enough to respond to the demands for skilled workers and trained personnel such a shift would entail. Thus business puts pressure on the

South African government to create a black skilled working-class, a relatively small segment of the black population which would be more stable, better educated, probably urbanized. Indeed, such a black skilled working-class has already begun to develop, often semi-legally, as business responds to market fluctuations.

This does not, of course, necessarily mean an end to apartheid as a basic means of control over the population; rather, apartheid could be extremely useful during the major social dislocations that such retooling of the economy would bring about. Further, industry still needs a plentiful supply of cheap unskilled labour for the foreseeable future; the bantustans not only supply this, but they provide a 'dumping ground' for those people industry no longer needs (the unemployed, sick, aged and very young) without the expense of a welfare system. But the business community has hoped government would adjust apartheid to cope with its new demands for skilled workers as well.

Both South African-based and trans-national corporations also have a vested interest in the success of South Africa's "constellation of states" foreign policy. Apartheid, paradoxically, curtails South African industry's internal markets by lowering the standard of living of much of the population; South African businesses look longingly at the markets of African states to the north. Independent African states, however, have shown an understandable reluctance to come openly within South Africa's sphere of influence. If South African businesses could point to an apparent improvement in the status of its black population, they might find a more enthusiastic welcome.

These changes are opposed by some white groups. The largest and most organized are the whites-only unions, which have a vested interest in limiting the potential size of the skilled working class to themselves. Many whites too have been wedded to a belief in cheap African labour for so long that they cannot accept the possibility of allowing some Africans to advance. Many whites fear they might lose the apparent privileges the system gives them, such as cheap domestic labour. The white government wavers between these two points of view. It believes in the necessity of rapid and, in traditional apartheid terms, fairly drastic change; on the other hand a white minority government cannot afford to totally alienate a large part of its (white) popular base.

It is impossible to judge how much projected change is honestly intended, and how much is mere window-dressing to appease the forces of change. Certainly some of the announced changes seem to take a very long time from conception to implementation, if they are implemented at all. Others appear purely imaginary from start to finish. But some of the apartheid laws have been altered, and many more may well follow. The purpose of this study is to examine more closely developments since 1976 and assess what is actually happening to the apartheid system.

*   *   *

Between the completion of this book at the end of 1979 and its publication, much has happened. At the level of detail some updating is needed and this is done in a postscript. But the basic analysis and the conclusions have been borne out. The upsurge of resistance across the country has expressed a clear and decisive rejection of the apartheid system in spite of the alleged reforms. And once again the regime, while carrying out a policy of ruthless repression, is announcing imminent changes in a continuation of the policies analysed in this paper.

Part One: Concessions?

We can be, and are, well on the way to achieving in my country equality
for all people before the law and equal chances and opportunities.
Dr. Piet Koornhof, Minister of Co-operation and Development,
speaking in the U.S., June 1979[1]

The P.W. Botha government claims that it is in the process of dismantling
apartheid. It says that it will allow Africans to own homes in the urban areas,
to vote for local (township) government, to work in any job and to join trade
unions. It says that it will give the townships electricity, that it will do away
with Bantu Education and that it will integrate sport. The record of actual
concessions certainly does not measure up to these sweeping claims. None the
less some changes have been made.

THE TOWNSHIPS

The Community Councils

The first moves towards "wooing the black middle class" were made by the
Vorster government. The Community Councils Act passed through Parliament
in July 1977. This Act claimed to give a form of "self-government" to the black
urban areas to parallel the "self-government" of the bantustans. The community
councils would become in theory black counterparts to the town councils of the
white areas. But urban Africans would never receive more than purely local
authority. The Prime Minister, Mr. Vorster, on introducing the Community
Council Bill in 1977, stated:

> . . . If people expect . . . that I must disengage the urban blacks from the
> blacks in the self-governing areas and that I must assimilate him into the
> white man's politics, I say to you that I am not prepared to do that, nor
> is it the mandate that I received from the electorate.
> . . . the white must gradually withdraw so that it may ultimately be black
> government in every respect, but this applies to local government.[2]

The original Community Councils Act empowered the Minister of Bantu
Affairs to set up community councils for any urban African residential area.
The size of the area is determined by the Minister. The number of members of
the council is determined by the Minister. The members of the council are
chosen by an electorate determined by the Minister in consultation with the
local Administration Board. The Minister may appoint council members to fill
any vacancies and the Minister can dissolve any community council whenever

he feels it 'in the public interest' to do so, or at the request of the local Administration Board after consultation with the community council.

The Community Councils Act gives the councils such powers as the Minister wishes to delegate to them, although these powers still remain "subject to the Minister's direction". Provision is made for the devolution of specific powers and duties, which may include: making recommendations to the authorities concerning the layout and renovation of the area and "other matters of interest to persons in the area"; making recommendations to the authorities concerned about educational matters; exercising all the "rights, powers, functions, duties and obligations" of an urban local authority that previously had been exercised by an Administration Board; and any other powers and functions the Minister so desires. The Minister may withdraw any such power or duty from a community council if he feels it necessary.

Powers specifically detailed in the Act include: "control over the keeping of dogs and the imposition of a levy for keeping of dogs, the promotion of sound community development in the area, the administration of sport, recreational and library services, and the award of bursaries".[3]

The councils are to be funded by such fines and levies as they can raise in the pursuit of their "duties", as well as any financial assistance the Ministry may donate. The Act makes provision for some judicial powers to devolve upon the community councils, and for creation of a "community guard". And to cement Ministerial control over the councils:

> The Minister may . . . make or apply regulations with regard to the mode of election to and vacating of offices by members of the Councils, the qualification required for voters and candidates for the Councils, the period of office, conditions of service, powers and duties of members of Councils, the convening procedure and conduct of meetings, the appointment, constitution, powers and duties of council committees, the employments, conditions of service and discharge of a council's staff, the control over the financial affairs of the council and *any other matters* at the discretion of the Minister[4] (*emphasis added*).

Urban African leaders commented that the Minister of Bantu Administration, Dr Connie Mulder, could have devolved such local government powers upon the previous Urban Bantu Advisory Boards if he had been so inclined, but he had not done so. Historically, South African governments had repeatedly offered Africans the privilege of electing representatives to a body that would advise the white government on how to treat Africans. The community councils follow the Urban Bantu Advisory Boards (of the 1960's) which followed the Native Representative Councils (1930's–40's). Many observers felt that the community councils were likely to remain within the established tradition, described as follows in 1946 before the Native Representative Council suspended itself and five years before it was finally abolished by the Nationalist Government:

> "We have been asked to co-operate with a toy telephone. We have been

speaking into an apparatus which cannot transmit sound and at the end of which there is nobody to receive the message".[5]

More important, even if the councils received full "local authority", they could only wield such authority within the framework of apartheid. They had no powers to challenge or change laws. For these reasons, Africans labelled the community councils a fraud, and boycotted them.

The first Soweto Community Council elections proceeded as follows. Out of 30 wards, 29 candidates were proposed, of whom 16 were disqualified by the West Rand Administration Board for unspecified reasons. Only two seats remained contested, with 9 unopposed and the remaining 19 seats were empty, to be filled by WRAB appointees or contested in a by-election. WRAB announced 200,000 Soweto residents had registered to vote as of 5 January 1978, but a week later they confessed that "voter registration" for community councils had been accomplished by including all house permit holders on the voter's roll.[6] Of the two contested wards, representing about six per cent of the Soweto electorate, only five per cent of those registered voted. The Soweto Community Council, then, was "elected" in the first instance by well under half of one per cent of those registered to vote. The man chosen as the Council's chairman, Mr. David Thebahali, won exactly 97 votes in all.[7] The then head of the Bantu-Administration Department, Dr. Connie Mulder, announced that these were "the democratically elected representatives of Soweto and the ones I will talk to".[8] The house of one of these two "elected representatives" was petrol-bombed the weekend of his electoral victory.

There is an interesting footnote to this. Mr. David Thebahali demanded a salary of R500 per month and ordinary community members asked for R300, on the grounds that they ran the risk of assault. They said: "We are not prepared to die for R30".[9] Eventually, they did receive pay rises pegged to the number of people in their ward. In Soweto ordinary members now receive R150 per month and the chairman gets R450 plus R100 entertainment allowance. Community councils have since requested minimum fees throughout the country, entertainment allowances for each member, and cars for the council chairman.[10]

In Soweto the by-elections two months later were little better. Despite police reinforcements around the polling booths, and pamphlets dropped by air on Soweto urging people to vote, only six per cent of the electorate turned out (3,600 out of 60,000 eligible voters). Of the 28 community council members (2 seats remained vacant), 12 were returned unopposed.[11]

In Mamelodi, Pretoria, in September 1978, the community council nominations left one seat contested out of ten, and two seats empty.[12] In Diepkloof and Meadowlands (Soweto) only 16 per cent of the electorate bothered to vote. In the model township of Daveyton, Benoni, in May, 1978, 20% of the electorate turned out. But significantly, in Dobsonville, Soweto, 42% of the electorate voted. The *Rand Daily Mail* explained editorially that Dobsonville is the "middle class" section of Soweto, with electricity, some security, rural wives

17

allowed residence, and so on and that people feel they have reason to participate in the official community institutions.[13]

Four days after the Dobsonville "elections", Mr. P. W. Botha became Prime Minister. The *Post* reported that the "general reaction from blacks . . . was one of disappointment and dismay".[14] But Mr. Botha's government drew the lesson from the Dobsonville results, that the government could only gain support from people who had something to lose.

Dr. Piet Koornhof the new Minister of Bantu Affairs (re-named Plural Relations and Development, and later Co-operation and Development), soon made it clear that he would devolve upon the community councils far greater powers than his predecessor apparently contemplated. Community councils have since been granted the right to issue licences in the townships for businesses; some have been given responsibility for the allocation of housing; some have received the right to negotiate loans from private sources; some have now received "tribal power" over some civil offences. (These last powers relating to civil offences are similar to those granted to chiefs and headmen in the Native Administration Act of 1927, giving them the right to enforce payment of fines and to imprison offenders within existing jails if the courts approve.)

These powers may not actually materialize fully for all community councils. Dr. Koornhof has reiterated that ". . . while we are fully committed to the concept of local government for blacks in their urban residential areas, we must understand that a process of evolution applies even here . . ."[15] These powers, as we have seen, remain under the direction of the Minister and may be removed by the Minister as he thinks fit.

But another serious catch exists in this "devolution" of powers. The community councils are merely enabled to administer the existing apartheid laws. They can in no way alter them. The community council will perhaps cease to be simply a "toy telephone", but instead it will become a tool to enforce the influx control regulations. It may give an illusion of self-government to the African township elite, but in return it will become the visible agent of the white government in the township. Previously, Administration Boards allocated housing, expelled squatters and took responsibility for the township roads and sewerage. As the community council takes over these functions, it may become the target of discontent as the body responsible for township conditions and the repression that goes with them. This could, to some extent, remove the (white) national government, which after all does control the basic framework in which a township must exist, from the direct line of fire.

A further and equally serious catch lies in the question of the economic position of the community councils. The councils were originally almost totally pensioners of the Ministry of Bantu Affairs, adding to this what revenue they received in the course of their duties (from dog licences, etc). With their new powers, their subsidy will be cut. According to the Deputy Minister:

. . . autonomy (for community councils) will come once the council is economically independent . . . the black man will therefore have to pay for his autonomy.[16]

The community councils will have to exist on rents, rates, licences and fines. One power that has not "devolved" upon the community council is that of running the Administration Board's liquor outlets, which provided between 40% and 66% of the Administration Boards' incomes in the year ending March 1977 (depending upon the board in question).[17] Further, African townships remain primarily "dormitory towns", with little business and no industry. Africans spend their money in white business districts and private enterprise at the moment plays practically no role in township revenues.

The community councils can only subsist on rents, rates, fines and licences if these go up drastically, as in fact they have done in the past few months. The councils will, therefore, not only administer the most hated apartheid laws but they will be, and are being, forced to increase the financial burden of the urban African. As Dobsonville Council "mayor" Steve Kgame announced when he introduced rent and rates increases of 200% (spread over a year from August 1979):

"The (Dobsonville) council accepted the unpleasant duty to ask the public to contribute to the rejuvenation of Dobsonville . . . The council realises that this places a heavy burden on the average householder."[18]

Drastic rent increases throughout the country would also follow from implementing some of the Riekert Commission of Inquiry's recommendations, discussed below.

In these ways Dr. Koornhof's Ministry hopes to make the councils viable. But Dr. Koornhof, like his predecessor, has affirmed that ". . . the political rights of the urban black would not be divorced from the bantustans and he would not obtain political rights in white South Africa."[19]

The Minister of Co-operation and Development has gone ahead in creating more community councils. By 6 July 1979, there were 168 councils established, of which 117 were functioning; 280 councils are planned in all.[20] An article in the *Financial Mail* claims the boycott is no longer effective: "Participation in council elections nevertheless seems to be picking up, with an average poll of 41%".[21] But this figure does not appear substantiated by the detailed returns that have been cited in the press: the first Cape Town council election in July 1979, for instance, polled 26% of the 19,000 eligible voters in the five contested wards, while ten wards were not contested.[22]

Home ownership schemes

Another of the Botha government's moves towards giving security to urban blacks was to implement a form of the urban black "home ownership" scheme. In theory, the Vorster government had accepted that such a scheme was necessary soon after the 1976 uprising, at least for Soweto. In practice, however, there was a succession of difficulties. Home ownership implies some form of claim to the land upon which the home stands and some rights to residence in

19

that home. This would contradict all the deepest laid tenets of Grand Apartheid: Africans must never have rights to land outside the bantustans.

The first "home ownership" scheme involved simply selling government-built houses to the resident, without any change in the laws governing residence. The cost of a Soweto house ran to about R1,700 (100% profit over the replacement cost) which could be paid monthly in instalments of R16 for 10 years.[23] If the "owner" missed an instalment, he could lose the house. He could also be "endorsed out" if he failed to meet any of the usual residence requirements (for instance if he lost his job). Moreover it was completely unclear whether his children would have any rights over the house if he died. Nothing at all was said about granting rights to the land upon which the house stood. Not surprisingly, the scheme met with little success. The final blow came with an exposé in the *Star* in November 1977: under Roman Dutch Law it turned out that the Bantu Administration Department's "sales" of houses failed to confer title to the house upon the buyer.[24] Building societies refused to recognise the sales or give loans for them.

In response the government gazetted a 99-year leasehold scheme under which the potential home owner could buy leasehold rights to the land, thus making his house title valid. The West Rand Administration Board also announced it would provide empty sites on which people could build their own houses—at a charge of R1000 extra per site, as a "contribution" to township infrastructure (roads, sewerage, running water and electricity (sic)). The East Rand Administration Board announced a similar arrangement at R400 per site.[25]

However, the Minister of Bantu Affairs, Dr. Mulder then muddied these unclear waters by stating expressly, in March 1978, that children of Africans who are "citizens of independent bantustans" could not inherit under the 99-year leasehold scheme.[26] Since in apartheid theory all Africans would eventually be "citizens of independent bantustans", presumably in far less than 99 years, this destroyed the security of tenure the 99-year leasehold supposedly created. The scheme was a concession to building societies, in no way a change in policy on African rights to the land in white areas.

By June 1978, only 38 of the 35,000 Mamelodi and Atteridgeville (Pretoria) families eligible for home ownership had applied to buy their homes (figures were not available for Soweto). The predictable happened in September 1978, when a Tembisa widow was evicted from a house for which she had paid all but R43 of the purchase price because she was a "Botswana national".[27]

The Botha government then gazetted a new, refined 99-year leasehold scheme for urban Africans, in December 1978. Africans would be allowed to buy the building, and the 99-year leasehold rights to the land, to occupy, build, and sell to any *qualified* person—with the Minister of Plural Relations retaining "discretion to determine if certain people are 'qualified' ".[28] Again the government had begged the key issue of the right to live on the land; the "owner" of the 99-year leasehold still had to obtain official approval to reside on his own plot. The *Sunday Post* commented:

What it means is that the Verwoerdian dictum remains inviolate because the majority of urban blacks are STILL excluded from any permanent stake in the urban areas. So the government has not really conceded anything at all, leaving us to draw the obvious conclusions.[29]

Four months later, the scheme actually got under way, with the question of the relationship between citizenship, ownership and residency still unresolved. The confusion can be seen clearly in Dr. Koornhof's statement in March 1979 that children of bantustan "citizens" *can* inherit houses bought under the new 99-year leasehold; however "people would only be eligible for the 99-year leasehold scheme if they qualified to be in urban areas by virtue of birth or period of residence".[30] Does this or does it not mean that someone who does not qualify in the first instance can inherit? The law as amended in 1978 merely reads: "A qualified person who is the holder of a registered right of leasehold and who, in the case of an African, ceases to be a qualified person of any provision of Section 10 (1) (a) or (b), or in the case of an association, ceases to be a qualified person, shall therefore *forfeit the right of occupation but not the right of leasehold*" (Act No. 25 of 1945, as amended 17 November 1978). Presumably at this point the owner's only right is that he may sell it.

In April 1979, the first lease was handed over to millionaire Richard Maponya, accompanied by front-page photos in all the township editions. By 1 May, this was still the only lease actually purchased, and only sixteen had been applied for. It turned out that the scheme so far was only open to Soweto's "luxury suburb" of Dube, because the West Rand Administration Board insisted upon the official WRAB surveyor surveying the plots to be sold first, and only Dube had been so surveyed.[31]

The financing of the 99-year leasehold scheme is another curious affair. The Urban Foundation, formed by a group of black and white businessmen, made available R30 million for home-ownership loans, to have an interest rate of 8.75% (as against the current South African interest rate of 10.5%). The money has been provided through loans from American banks, made for a five year period only, "after which it is hoped black incomes will have risen sufficiently to permit borrowers to pay the going SA rate without undue hardship . . .". According to the Urban Foundation, this lower rate of interest would enable 75% of Soweto families to buy thir houses.[32]

The Urban Foundation calculated this on the basis that a family with a minimum monthly income of R128 would qualify for a loan under this scheme. But an income of R128 per month is well below the breadline for Soweto: the minimum living level was R162 a month when these loans were made available—below the R162 line a family went without basic necessities such as food, clothing, or fuel. A family with an income of R128 simply could not afford the monthly payments, even though in theory they could obtain a loan.

A R5,000 loan, for the cheapest Soweto house plus R1,000 improvement, becomes available to a family with a monthly income of R156 when "the monthly repayment on a R5,000 loan over 30 years would be roughly R39, money that would cut into the living standard of the family to the extent of producing malnutrition".[33] One survey in 1977 calculated that the average urban African household of 6.36 people had an income (from all wage-earners in the family) of R158 per month. In the same year the minimum living level for Soweto was calculated for a family of five at R150 per month. The average family can barely afford to survive, much less pay back a housing loan.

The 75% of Soweto families who qualify for an Urban Foundation loan have not queued up for them. In July 1979 building societies complained that no one had applied for the loans they made available.[34] By October 1979, "no more than a meagre 14 families have registered such (99-year leasehold) titles since the scheme was introduced several months ago".[35]

The Urban Foundation recently reacted to complaints that slowness in surveying the sites held up the leasehold scheme. In an attempt to remove this block, they made a loan of R500,000 to the Department of Co-operation and Development to survey land for 99-year leasehold plots. This loan, unlike loans to potential plot buyers, was completely interest free. The *Financial Mail* asserted that this would open the bottleneck preventing the scheme from operating successfully.[36]

It should be pointed out that, since the majority of the urban African population cannot afford to buy their homes on a 99-year leasehold, these schemes benefit only the small number of people who can afford it. This will be so even if the questions still unsettled about citizenship and residence, not to mention the lack of title for houses "owned" under the home ownership scheme are resolved in the least restrictive way. The Administration Boards, over the last two decades, have severely limited the number of houses built in African townships to way below the demand for accommodation, as one of the mechanisms of enforcing influx control. Thus, the waiting list in Soweto for a house is nine years long, yet WRAB only built 422 houses there in 1977. 401 of these were sold under the home ownership scheme and only 21 were let.[37]

People who have been on the list since 1970 are told that they will never get a house unless they buy one, and most do not earn enough to make that even a remote possibility. They are presently watching with bitterness the wealthy who can afford to buy, jumping the queue.[38]

Other Improvements

Several other improvements in the living conditions of Soweto, if not the other townships across South Africa, seem to be going forward.

Soweto has no electricity. Coal is used for heating and cooking, paraffin lamps and candles for light. The coal-smog in the winter becomes a serious health-hazard, blanketing the township in cloud. After the 1976 uprising, a consortium of liberal banks organized by Mr. Harry Oppenheimer (head of the Anglo-American Corporation) offered to provide a loan of R59 million to install electricity in Soweto. The loan was to be for five years, at the normal rate for short term loans of 13% interest.[39] The parliamentary Opposition lauded this as a step to improve life in Soweto. The Vorster Government turned down the offer, on the not totally specious grounds that it was a profit-making venture, not particularly philanthropic, and as such should be put out to tender. However for the next two years, despite continuous reminders that Soweto needed electricity, the government dragged its feet and inflation forced the projected costs of installing electricity up to R94 million.[40]

Finally the Soweto Community Council took up the issue (probably to prove their own effectiveness as a form of local government). First, they conducted a poll of the Soweto population, to see if a significant proportion really would prefer electricity. WRAB had proposed such a poll in August 1978. It was conducted in December 1978, and showed overwhelming support for the introduction of electricity. However, it was reported that "the whole issue of electricity for Soweto was still with WRAB"—the community council did not apparently have the power to make the decision. In particular, the community councils did not have the power to negotiate loans independently: it was not until March 1979 that the Ministry of Plural Relations transferred additional powers to them to enable them to proceed with such negotiations.[41] The Soweto Community Council chairman, David Thebahali, signed the first loan agreement for R20 million in August 1979, as the first instalment of the eventual cost of R150 million over the next five years. He announced that "the digging of trenches for cables was expected to begin within the next two weeks".[42]

In early 1979 the Post Office brought more telephones to Soweto. By 1981, they plan to install 14,000 new lines compared to the 200 previously in use.[43]

One should remember that this only refers to Soweto. Other townships continue dark and smog-ridden. A typical example of the functioning of other townships is the grandiose plan announced for Edenvale (Pietermaritzburg), calling for the building of "10 creches, 2 tennis courts, a swimming pool and an orphanage" and for "a local fund to help people to install water and electricity as well as providing low interest loans for black entrepreneurs". The impression fades rather as the plan discusses financial realities, with an "appeal to white commerce and industry for both expertise and funds", which if donated would be administered by a joint committee representing the Advisory Boards, the Rotary Club, and the Urban Foundation.[44]

Township Commercial Services

Another projected change in township life is an improvement in retail business facilities. Until the last few years black businessmen operated under severe restrictions. They were unable to own more than one type of business, unable to own a business in an area they themselves were not resident in, unable to employ people of a different race and so on. White businessmen were not permitted to own businesses in black areas in terms of the Group Areas Act. As a result townships had practically no business beyond the small corner store level, and most major shopping required a trip to the white city centre.

23

Recently the restrictions on black businessmen operating within black areas have been largely removed (*see later*). In Soweto, the National African Chamber of Commerce (NAFCOC) has begun building a supermarket costing R1.5 million, with a larger one planned to follow in Jabulani (Soweto). White businessmen have also responded to this potentially gigantic market, planning a R21 million supermarket on white land next to Soweto. This was temporarily suspended by Dr. Mulder, as head of the Department of Bantu Affairs, following complaints by NAFCOC, but now appears to be going forward. The township market has been further opened to white enterprise with the announcement by Dr. Koornhof in November 1979 that whites will be allowed to form partnerships with African businessmen in African areas, as long as the white share is under 49% of the business. African entrepreneurs fear that white penetration of the townships, with the far greater resources white enterprise can command, will rob them of their markets. The government's response was that "an improvement in commercial services in Soweto will help improve the quality of life".[45]

Another possible improvement in township "services" may come about in the near future with the legalizing of shebeens. At the moment only the Administration Board outlets (beerhalls) may serve liquor legally in the townships. Illegal bars however have a long and celebrated history. In July 1979 Soweto police began a campaign to enforce a law subjecting shebeen patrons to R500 fines and/or 6 months in prison. Shebeen owners responded with a boycott of WRAB liquor outlets. WRAB outlets emptied and the police campaign ended.[46] Police have since called for a legal African-owned liquor system in the townships.[47]

The New "Black Education"

The Department of Education and Training (previously Bantu Education) announced in 1978 that it would eliminate "Bantu Education", which had caused the school boycott of 1976-1978 and touched off the 1976 uprising. They claimed that they would replace Bantu Education with a new form of "blacks only" education. They were aiming, they said, at eventually producing compulsory education for blacks in "selected areas for defined pupils". This was very far from universal compulsory education, and even then it would not be free.[48] In February 1979 the Minister of Education and Training, Mr. P. Jansen, specified that "compulsory education for black pupils was practically and financially impossible for at least the next two years".[49] The curriculum would undergo some changes, the most significant being the introduction of English or Afrikaans as a medium of instruction from Standard 4. Some textbooks, at least at secondary level, would be supplied free.

Black educationalists and church and political leaders immediately attacked this new "black education". One fact makes nonsense of the whole scheme: the Department of Education and Training did not intend to change the amount spent per child for the new "improved" black education. In 1976/77 the government spent R48 for a black education and R654 for a white child's education.

"There is simply no way that a R50-a-year education can be even vaguely compared with a R650-a-year operation".[50]

Further evidence of the unreliability of the new Department of Education and Training came with the end of the 1976 school boycott, in January 1979. Since 1976 all black education had been somewhat sporadic, with secondary schools in particular practically continuously disrupted. Many Soweto secondary schools had not operated properly since 1976 and several were in ruins. The Soweto Students Representative Council, which had organized the original boycott, went underground and its leaders went to jail or were shot or fled abroad. Its successor, a group called the Soweto Students' League, continued the boycott but avoided confrontation, organizing memorial meetings for the dead rather than mass demonstrations. The SSL leaders also met with detention and exile.

But in January 1979, with the new Minister for Plural Relations promising an end to Bantu Education, which would have been a victory for the students, the school boycott was called off for a year. The SSL, at a meeting of 2,000 pupils and parents at Soweto's Regina Mundi Cathedral, urged students to go back, against "strong opposition" by some of those present.[51] SSL Chairman E. Maphana spelled out their position:

"By saying students must go to school, we want to show the government we are non-violent. We are giving them a chance to put their house in order as they promised".[52]

Five days after this statement, as the schools opened without protest, security police detained Mr. Maphana.[53]

The end of the boycott revealed how little the Department of Education and Training had done to improve the situation. Schools damaged during the riots were not rebuilt. Instead students were jammed into what classrooms there were, fitting up to 60 pupils in rooms built for 45. Primary schools doubled up with secondary schools.[54] The Department of Education and Training, obviously caught unprepared by the end of the boycott, was still trying to place Soweto secondary school students in schools a month and a half after the term had officially begun.[55] The Department claimed it planned to spend R2.4 million on construction and repair of Soweto schools.[56] At least this appeared to be an improvement over the previous Minister of Bantu Education's announcement that they would not replace damaged schools at all. Whether the government produces this money or not remains to be seen: what is clear is that in terms of school buildings, the situation in Soweto for the 1979 school year appeared well below even the standards of pre-1976 Bantu Education.

In terms of the improvement in township conditions there is clearly a great need to replace damaged schools, to provide new ones and to raise the level of facilities—laboratories, libraries, sports grounds—which were rarely provided in "Bantu" schools. The government appears to acknowledge the need for large-scale expenditure in this area but at the same time is reluctant to authorise it, believing that the African communities should produce the funds for their "own" services. As a result, money for education is coming from private

25

enterprise which is financing school building through such bodies as the Urban Foundation.

Emphasis has also been placed on the need for higher levels of technical education for Africans, and the Education and Training Act recognized this. This is dealt with in a later section, together with alterations in the status of African workers.

RACE SEPARATION

As well as taking various steps in regard to the status of and conditions in the African townships, there have also been official statements about the general principles of racial segregation which underpin apartheid, namely the prohibitions on social mixing and intermarriage. These are the subject of much debate.

Petty Apartheid

Another move to improve the quality of life for the black elite has been the "removal" of petty apartheid (simple segregation of facilities such as restaurants, washrooms, and trains) in some areas.

In 1975 the government agreed that the few hotels designated as "International Status" establishments would be allowed to give rooms to black guests, and serve them with liquor if they were bonafide hotel residents or guests of hotel residents. Africans would still not be permitted to dance at such hotels. Of course there was an economic barrier preventing most black South Africans from taking advantage of this opportunity since such hotels tend not to be cheap. In case such barriers failed the Liquor Board and hotel licencees made a "private" agreement to limit the number of South African blacks (as opposed to foreign Africans or black Americans) allowed at "International Status" hotels.[1] Moreover the government specifically warned such hotels that they must not knowingly allow couples of different races to share bedrooms, or they would face charges under the Immorality Act.[2] In practice, this means a white married abroad to a black is not allowed to stay at such a hotel with his or her spouse, even in separate rooms, since it would be a reasonable assumption that they would breach the Immorality Act. However a white and a black who are not married and who arrive together but do not officially share a bedroom are allowed to register.

Restaurants and sports clubs also may apply for International Status, which enables them to serve wines and beers to African guests, although not hard liquor.[3] In July 1978 only six restaurants had attained International Status in all of South Africa, as well as 71 sports clubs and 58 hotels.[4] In other words, in all of South Africa in July 1978, the population of 24 million Africans and whites could eat and drink publicly together in exactly 135 places.

This record has not improved greatly. By January 1980 only 3 restaurants in Johannesburg (excluding hotels) had been granted International Status although other restaurants occasionally broke the law by serving Africans. The chairman of the Johannesburg Central Business Association was quoted as saying: "The general attitude of the board was that Government policy was for separate restaurants . . ." He said Government policy towards liquor permits was also deceptive . . . Although the Minister of Community Development, Mr. Steyn, has relaxed the requirements for unlicensed premises to serve blacks, he did not know of any premises in Johannesburg with such exemptions.[5]

In September 1979, the Minister of Community Development Mr. S. J. Steyn announced that restaurants would not have to re-apply for International Status permits annually, but could be granted permanent international status. Such permits could, of course, still be removed by the Minister at his discretion.[6]

The Government introduced, in 1978, a permit system by which persons of different races could attend live performances in certain theatres. The conditions state the performance must be live, while the relevant local authority and the theatre owner both have to sign statements that they have no objections. Further, the theatre has to show a minimum number of performances a year to qualify. The Minister grants those permits at his own discretion and can withdraw them at any time.

In June 1978, 26 out of 30 applications for theatre permits were accepted (12 in Johannesburg, 4 in Durban, 2 each in Cape Town, Stellenbosch, and Pietermaritzburg and one each in George, Somerset West, Port Elizabeth and Grahamstown). No Pretoria applications could be considered since the Pretoria City Council refused to countenance the applications.[7]

In December 1979 the South African government announced it would allow a "wide range of public facilities, including private hospitals, theatres and restaurants" to apply for indefinite permits to serve people from all races, instead of separate permits for individual events or limited periods of time. The London Guardian headlined this "South Africa eases race barriers", and cited the Prime Minister's pledge to "eliminate petty apartheid".[8] But these permits only exempt specific enterprises from the petty apartheid laws (which have not been changed) and of course they remain subject to the Minister's discretion.

The "elimination of petty apartheid" in other fields looks equally questionable.

Petty apartheid has in theory been removed from railways in the Western Cape. This means that "whites only" signs were removed. But First Class remains for whites only, excepting a few First Class cars specifically reserved for blacks, and third class remains for blacks only.[9]

All "whites only" signs have also been removed from the airports (domestic as well as international).

The parliamentary opposition suggested desegregating buses in Johannesburg or else instituting "in-bus apartheid" instead of having totally segregated buses, in order to conserve fuel (since "whites only" buses tend to be relatively empty). In 1979 however the Johannesburg City Council turned the idea down.[10]

In December 1978, "nearly half" the Cape Peninsula beaches were reported to be desegregated—while apartheid was more strictly enforced on the others. Opening some beaches to all races was attacked as "an excuse to enforce beach apartheid more rigidly".[11]   On Boxing Day, 1979, "more than 500 people were warned off "white" beaches in the Peninsula . . .   The police had reacted to complaints from the public and also had orders to patrol the beaches".[12]

The much-advertised removal of petty apartheid has therefore not materialized.   Where facilities have been exempted from racial segregation, they are usually far too expensive for the majority of the African population to afford. High-class restaurants, hotels and theatres do not fall within the economic range of most of the black people in South Africa.

The Immorality Act

One suggestion of "concession" which received world-wide attention for its symbolic value was Prime Minister Botha's assertion that he would consider altering the Immorality Act, which bars sex between people of different races.

> "Mr. Botha (said) . . . that he was prepared to consider constructive suggestions for revision of the section of the Immorality Act which forbids miscegenation and the Prohibition of Mixed Marriages Act".[13]

If the Immorality Act were repealed, it is probable that it would not directly affect large numbers of people: in the calender year of 1976 351 persons were prosecuted under the Act, of whom 260 were convicted.[14]   Courts have been increasingly reluctant to sentence people severely, giving only suspended or postponed sentences.   On the other hand, the Act has been pointed to as the epitome of racial intolerance by South Africa's enemies, and its retention could undermine South Africa's "new image".   But it is also linked to residential segregation, petty apartheid and rights of property ownership and inheritance. It is inconceivable that the state would sanction the repeal of the Immorality Act while retaining the Prohibition of Mixed Marriages Act and thus make inter-racial sexual intercourse outside marriage legal, but illegal within it, as this would go against the teaching of the church.

The response to Mr. Botha's speech by the National Party was very strong and very negative.   Opinion polls showed that less than 30% of the Party favoured scrapping the Immorality Act, and less than 25% favoured scrapping the Prohibition of Mixed Marriages Act.[15]   Within a month the government had:

> embarked on a full-scale attempt to reassure right-wing voters that the Prime Minister does not support the repeal of the Immorality Act and the Mixed Marriages Act.[16]

A large advertisement in the National Party paper *Die Transvaler* quoted the Prime Minister as saying he wished to "improve" the act, not "eliminate" it:

> It is therefore wrong to say that the Prime Minister talked about abolition (of the Act). He explicitly talked about improvement.[17]

At the opening session of the 1980 parliamentary session Mr. Botha specifically stated the Act would remain.[18]

Sport

One of the main "concessions" to the African population, the government claims, has been the development of "multi-national" sport.

From 1956 onwards government policy stated that Africans, Coloureds, Asians and whites should organise sports completely separately, with no sports competition allowed between races. Black organisations, if they so desired, could seek international recognition and involvement under the aegis of the appropriate white sports organisations. Because of this policy, South Africa was excluded from nearly all international sports competitions.

In 1967, Prime Minister Vorster announced that a mixed team would be created for the Olympics, although no mixed sport would be tolerated internally. This failed to mollify the Olympics committee, and South Africa remained excluded.

In 1976, the Government promulgated a new sports policy, under the leadership of Dr. Piet Koornhof, then Minister of Sport and Recreation. This policy permitted sportsmen to compete against each other as representatives of one group ("nation") against another. It was designated "multi-national" sport, as opposed to "multi-racial" sport. The government encouraged "multi-national" sport in individual but not team contests. Teams sent overseas would represent their own "ethnic group". Only whites would carry the national Springbok colours.

The question of the legality of racially mixed sport at club, provincial or national level became a very vexed issue. Dr. Koornhof in August 1976 said in a Department of Information publication with overseas distribution: "There is no law prohibiting mixed race clubs in any sport in South Africa". On another occasion, though, he pointed out that "mixed sport at club level remains contrary to party policy", and illustrated this with a Department of Sport survey showing that by the end of June 1976 there were only 56 cases of whites playing for black clubs or vice versa, of which 31 cases were in cricket. This, he asserted with approval, represented 0.0045% of the sports-playing population. A week later Dr. Koornhof stated that multi-national sport was free from discrimination on the basis of race and colour, and a week after that statement he claimed it was "an infamous lie" to say Government policy on sport had changed.[19]

The Transvaal Education Department in 1978 sent a circular to all public and publicly-aided private schools (all white) emphasizing that sports between black and white schools was "not desirable". Exemptions permitting such matches would however be considered if the application for exemption met the approval of school boards and principals in consultation with circuit inspectors and governing bodies. In 1978 the Cape authorities accepted all 13 such requests for matches between black and white schools.[20]

The Minister of Community Development in August 1976, stated that since mixed sports clubs had to apply for permits, the situation was a "very elastic" one dependent upon his department's decisions.

By the end of the year it was generally accepted that mixed sport at club level was not illegal except as it might be affected by the liquor laws, the Group Areas Act, and the Reservation of Separate Amenities Act, but that it still remained contrary to National Party policy.[21]

In other words, multi-racial sporting contests are legal (if not encouraged) provided: that participants and spectators are specially invited and pay no admission; that the event is held on private land with the owner's permission, or on public fields with official permission; that, if a public event, separate toilets are available; and that a permit is issued for use of a club house.

In February 1978 Dr. Koornhof stated that players of different races would not require Group Areas Act permits to play against each other and that a permit for a sports club to admit all races as spectators would be granted for one year at a time. Sports clubs could also apply for International Status if they wished to curcumvent the liquor laws. By May, 188 clubs had applied for International Status[22] and by August, between 70 and 80 applications had been granted.

No actual law forbids mixed teams on a local level. However, when eight white players joined black teams for a game in Port Elizabeth in 1976, they were threatened with discipline by white sports officials. One player, who coached a black team as well as playing with them, was arrested and charged with being in a black area without a permit. He was cautioned and discharged.[23]

The "multi-national" solution envisaged by the National Party is visible in the South African Rugby Board. The SARB, which was previously for whites only, accepted as Board members three delegates each from African and Coloured unions. Each group also contibuted two teams to participate in the 1978 competitions.[24] A mixed team composed of players from separate African, Coloured and white team associations played in the first mixed inter-provincial match in August 1978. In February 1978 the SARB announced that rugby clubs could if they wished open their doors to members of all races: few clubs appeared to accept members of mixed races following this announcement.

Soccer games played between teams of different races have ended in rioting on several occasions, "caused, among other things, by inadequate facilities and by what were seen as biased decisions by white referees. Security fences were erected at a number of grounds".[25] Police used batons and dogs to quell fans.

"Multi-national" sport has another catch for Africans who officially participate as representatives of their "nations". When their "bantustan" becomes an independent state, they no longer qualify for South African citizenship and thus cannot carry South African colours. In late 1979 the Government barred Mathews Motswanatu, who set the South African record for the 800 metres, from carrying Springbok colours on the grounds that he was a BophuthaTswana citizen. (In protest, Johnnie Halberstadt, an internationally famous marathon runner, also refused to accept Springbok colours.[26])

As in other areas, apartheid remains unchallenged in the financing of sport. The following amounts were appropriated for sports and recreation by the respective bodies controlling sport for each race for the year ending 31 March 1979:

Department of Sport & Recreation (white)   R2,624,000   (86.6%)
Department of Plural Relations & Devel.   R   127,000   (4.19%)
Department of Coloured Relations   R   100   (0.003%)
Department of Defence   R   279,000   (9.21%)[27]

These constitute the central government's contributions to sports for the different races.

The Minister of Plural Relations has claimed that his Ministry spent R10 million on black sport in the same period The Minister of Sport claims that the government spent almost R12 million on black sport, R5.5 million on Coloured sport, and only R2½ million on white sport. The explanation of the extremely wide differences between appropriations and claims lies in the fact that official figures of government expenditures do not include money spent by provincial administrators and municipalities—money which can come from their own sources. For blacks, sport is primarily financed not by government contributions but by money creamed off the black population by the Administration Boards and, more recently, community councils, money gained from local sports and liquor outlets, for instance, and spent on a municipal level. A breakdown for the West Rand Administration Board's finances, for example, shows an estimated income of R525,000 from "Sport etc", and an estimated expenditure of R900,000 on sport.[28] As has been mentioned earlier, 40% of WRAB's total income comes from liquor. Blacks pay for black sport, via the administration boards; the central government pays for white sport.

This disparity in financing is reflected in the official figures for those taking part in various sports. In 1978 the following statistics were given of black/white sport participation:

	White	*African*
Cricket	40,120	1,544
Swimming	12,000	1,164
Squash	18,000	15[29]

This shows how sport in an apartheid society reflects the character of that society. The "concessions" the government has made in sport serve to underline the built-in racial divisions that cut through the structure, financing and playing of South African sport. These concessions only create exceptions to the rule of racially segregated sport. They do not eliminate it.

POLITICAL POWER

Simultaneously with the moves discussed above to improve the image of apartheid, there have been claims that South Africa is moving towards a "new political dispensation" not based on racial dominance. This does not envisage any kind of "power-sharing" but various forms of consultation and co-option.

31

Consultation with African Leaders

The verligte Minister of Co-operation and Development (ex-Plural Relations, ex-Bantu Affairs) proposed in May 1979 that he would consult "regional committees" containing the more influential of the legal black South African leaders in the urban areas, men considered relatively moderate by the liberation movements, but dangerously liberal by previous South African governments. These included such men as Dr. Motlana, head of the Committee of Ten, a self-appointed body composed of prominent Soweto civic leaders. It also included some of those who would be considered, from an establishment point of view, to be the most respectable voices of protest in Soweto, such as Percy Qoboza, editor of the *Post* (and previously editor of the now banned *World*) and also a member of the Commitee of Ten, and the Anglican Bishop Desmond Tutu, head of the South African Council of Churches and an outspoken critic of apartheid. On the same consulting body would sit such men as the head of the Soweto Community Council, Mr. David Thebahali. Dr. Koornhof did not guarantee to accept any advice given by this body and merely said he would consult it. He did not propose to weigh their advice with considerations of their very different bases of support.

The Soweto Committee of Ten showed indecision at first over whether it should join this advisory committee. The *Post*'s editor urged in his columns that "serious thought" should be given to accepting the invitation. However, the Committee of Ten finally decided unanimously not to join. It was perhaps tempting for the Committee of Ten to feel the government would finally listen to them, as Soweto's top civic leaders (and par excellence the "black middle class" the government hopes to win to its side), but the Committee also made it clear that they had no wish to be "listened to" on the same committee as Mr. David Thebahali, who won his seat as Head of the Soweto Community Council with only 97 votes.[1]

Similar liaison committees proposed for other parts of South Africa provoked a similar response from African townships. The government expressed "disappointment" when nearly all black leaders turned down the offer of talks except for some generally regarded as compromised by a record of cooperation with apartheid. That the rejection was in tune with the mood of the black population, however, is reflected in the fact that in the early part of 1979, the "mayor" of Mamelodi Community Council had to flee from the crowd when he attempted to "report back" to the people following discussions he held with the Deputy Minister of Plural Relations.[2]

The few politically independent Africans who did join the regional committees resigned. Rev. Sam Buti, the popular leader of the fight to save Alexandra township from demolition, stated upon his resignation:

> I could not continue my membership without jeopardizing my integrity . . .
> In principle, nothing new has been presented, no real or meaningful change
> is presented or envisaged. In fact, apartheid is alive and kicking—but only

in a more subtle and sophisticated fashion. This whole exercise is meaningless...[3]

Prof. C. L. S. Nyembezi (one of Chief Gatsha Buthelezi's Inkatha movement advisors) resigned from the Durban-Pietermaritzburg regional committee claiming that ". . . the problem facing the committee was that its recommendations had to take into account the government's policy of apartheid".[4]

The New Constitution: the "New Deal" for Coloureds and Indians

Another major aspect of the Botha government's plan to save South Africa is the "new deal" to be offered to Coloureds and Indians. Unlike the African population these groups have no "homelands" to which they may be sent and eventually, if South Africa wishes to evade world condemnation, some "solution" will have to be promulgated for them. In 1976, the Cabinet appointed a Committee chaired by the then Minister of Defence, Mr. P. W. Botha (now Prime Minister), to investigate "possible and desirable adjustments to the existing constitutional order . . . in respect of the two political systems for the Coloured and Indian communities".[5] The resulting constitutional plan had been endorsed by the four white National Party provincial congresses, rejected by the Coloured Representative Council (albeit by the chairman's casting vote), and rejected unanimously by the South African Indian Council.[6] Nonetheless in April 1979 it was put as a bill before the (white) parliament. The government appeared surprised by the amount of opposition its proposals provoked.

The new constitution will totally exclude Africans from the national government. Indeed the preamble to the New Constitution reads:

"IN HUMBLE SUBMISSION to Almighty God, Who controls the destinies of nations and the history of people,

Who gathered our forebears together from many lands and gave them this their own;

Who has guided them from generation to generation;

Who has wondrously delivered them from the dangers that beset them;

"We DECLARE that whereas we

"ARE CONSCIOUS of our responsibility towards God and man;

"BELIEVE that the black nations of the Republic should each be given separate freedom in the land allotted to them for the exercise of the political aspirations of all the members of those nations . . ."

This establishes (by Act of Parliament) that God gave South Africa to the whites. Africans may enjoy their "separate freedom in the land allotted to them".[7]

This Constitution Bill proposed a government consisting primarily of a State President and three separate "parliaments", one for whites (the "Assembly"), one for Coloured people (the "House of Representatives") and one for Indians (the "Chamber of Deputies"). Each group would elect their "own" parliaments separately.

The State President would then be chosen by an electoral college composed of fifty members of the (white) Assembly, 25 members of the (Coloured) House of

Representatives, and thirteen members of the (Indian) Chamber of Deputies. The whites thus outvote the other two groups by 50 to 38 (proportions are based approximately on population size).

The State President so elected then appoints three Prime Ministers and three sets of Ministers, one set for each group (6 white Ministers, 3 Coloured and 2 Indian), which sitting together make up the Council of Cabinets. The State President may dismiss any minister or Prime Minister at will, after consultation with the relevant Prime Minister. (Even without considering the President's powers of dismissal, the white members of the Council of Cabinets balance the non-white members; the State President sits in the chair and presumably holds the decisive vote.)

The President also has a council consisting of 55 members appointed by the president to advise the Council of Cabinets.

Beyond all this, only the (white) assembly has power to pass legislation, excepting the powers vested in the Coloured Representative Council which will be transferred to the (Coloured) House of Representatives, and those of the Indian Council which will be vested in the (Indian) Chamber of Deputies. The powers of the Coloured Representative Council and the Indian Council included such matters as "finance, local government, education, and community development . . ." as they affected Coloureds and Indians respectively. But all financing had to meet the approval of the Ministers of Coloured and Indian Affairs, as well as the Ministry of Finance; and after that their budgets were approved by the white Parliament. (As with the community councils these bodies could only implement apartheid; they had no power to change it.)

In the new constitution, the Council of Cabinets may if it wishes confer additional powers upon the House of Representatives and the Chamber of Deputies. The Council of Cabinets may further refer proposed legislation that would affect Indians and Coloureds to their respective parliaments; if these parliaments reject the legislation, the Council of Cabinets may reconsider the matter. However, if there is no agreement, the State President shall decide if the legislation shall be put into effect.

All bills must be submitted to the State President.

No court of law may enquire into the validity of any Act passed by the new government.

Thus, under the new constitution, there are three nominally separate parliaments, but they are in fact neither separate nor equal. The white Assembly has an overwhelming majority (50 to 38) in the electoral college that chooses the State President. The State President in turn appoints "Ministers" and "Prime Ministers" for each group, whom he can dismiss at will. And only the white Assembly can pass legislation; the State President makes the final decisions on legislation affecting the other two groups.

The drafting of the new constitution leaves the question of control over Africans extremely vague (although, as we saw, it speaks very precisely about

34

their exclusion from the land and the new government). The constitution states:

> The control and administration of black affairs and of matters specially or differentially affecting Asians throughout the Republic shall vest in the State President, who shall exercise all those special powers in regard to black administration which immediately prior to the commencement of this Act were vested in him . . .[8]

The constitution does not detail the bureaucracy by which the State President shall exercise these powers. The new constitution announces also (as practically all new constitutions must) that all existing laws except those specifically discussed in its provisions shall continue as before. So for the African population nothing will change.

The new Constitution Bill met with major opposition and was referred to a parliamentary select committee under Minister of Justice Schlebusch.

Since then, opposition has continued to grow. Indian leaders after some debate have called for a boycott of the proposed Chamber of Deputies, and "dialogues" between Mr. Botha and Labour Party leaders (the largest Coloured party) ended in "bitter dispute". The Labour Party demanded universal suffrage (including Africans), and representation of all peoples in a single parliament; Mr. Botha rejected this outright.

Mr. Botha also warned Labour Party leaders that "if it did not co-operate with him he would have to find Coloured leaders who would".[9] Early in 1980 the Coloured Representative Council was abolished.

THE ECONOMIC SPHERE

In the economic sphere, a number of "concessions" have also been projected for some sections of the black population, in a way which represents the Botha government's perception that some level of support has to be won from the black population, preferably to reduce their commitment to the aims of the liberation struggle and in any case to persuade the outside world that South African society is not based on crude racial exclusion.

Instead, the picture to be presented is of a society in which blacks can advance themselves economically and socially through the free enterprise system. And in order to be convincing, this picture must have some basis in reality.

Most of the projected improvements to apartheid presume a certain level of income in at least part of the black urban population. A home ownership scheme for Africans is of no use where no African can afford to buy a house. International Status restaurants will serve only whites if no Africans can pay their prices. Electricity may cost less than coal, but it requires extra investment in electric stoves and fixtures, as well as installation fees. The new Black Education will not be free—and parents are further expected to pay for uniforms and books (textbooks are free only in Soweto). These concessions all aim expressly at the richer urban African, the "black middle class".

However, this black middle class hardly exists as yet. Apartheid (until recently) severely hampered the black businessman: the "Soweto tycoon" so built up in the South African press owns no more than a few corner grocery stores or garages. African "professionals" have been limited by the structure of Bantu Education as well as the job market: in the townships, a hospital nurse occupies a highly prestigeous position, as does a secondary school teacher. And the job colour bar by law has kept African workers in unskilled and low paying jobs in industry. Indeed, the percentage of Africans in the "middle class" job categories has dropped between 1970 and 1978, due primarily to world recession (Africans are last hired and first fired), but due also to the cumulative impact of Bantu Education. The percentage of Africans (compared to the total population) in the category of "administrative, executive and managerial personnel" dropped from 2.9% to 0.4%; in "Professional, semi-professional and technical staff" from 29% to 26%; in "Artisans" from 2.5% to 2.1%; and in "Clerical workers" from 13.4% to 13.2%.[6]

It has become increasingly clear that if the government intends to "woo the black middle class", it must first alter the structure of apartheid enough to permit this black middle class to emerge.

The Black Businessman

The main move in this direction has been the elimination of many of the restrictions on black businessmen. On 22 September 1978 the government removed many of the legal barriers to black businessmen operating in black areas. Previously an African could not own more than one business, he had to be resident in the same area that the business was in and he could only own very limited types of business. Moreover he could not own a business site over 350 sq. m. and he had to employ persons of the same race as himself. All of these restrictions were dropped.[2]

A year later, (November 1979) Dr. Koornhof announced the relaxation of some of the remaining restrictions. The government gave its approval to black-white partnerships on a 51% black, 49% white basis, to be enforced by government watch-dogs. Immediate projects approved for black-white business collaboration include construction of a large commercial business centre in Soweto and an industrial complex there.[3]

Recently, white businessmen have gone further: Anton Rupert in November 1979 offered R5 million towards a R100 million fund to set up small businesses mainly for Africans.[4]

African businessmen have still not reached a legally equal basis with white businessmen. They must still operate within African areas only, thus remaining barred from the far better facilities and infrastructures available to whites. Because of the leasehold complications an African business still has great difficulty in getting a mortgage. Africans do not have equal training facilities; in 1979 there were only two African MBAs in all of South Africa.[5] The Government still has some way to go before it reaches its stated goals, expressed in remarks like this one by the Prime Minister's Economic Adviser: "Blacks must be allowed to take part fully in the free enterprise system if we want them to accept it and defend it and make it their own. They must have a vested interest in it".[6]

The black elite and the Wiehahn Report

The white government is under pressure to do more than create a few token black businessmen. The whole cheap labour-intensive system that apartheid was created to support is under threat. With the curtailment of the migrant labour supply from the liberated north, and with unrest among the black majority at home, industry has begun to look towards increased mechanization and capital-intensive techniques. These require a skilled, if smaller, working class. The apartheid system has traditionally strictly limited skilled jobs to the white population; under the "old" apartheid the skilled working class could not expand to meet the demands that capital-intensive processes would generate.

The government's response to this came in February 1979, in the Report of the Commission of Inquiry into Labour Legislation, popularly known as the Wiehahn Report. It constitutes the first official study of labour practices in South Africa in thirty years. In the introduction to the Wiehahn Report, it is stated that a major reason for the report was:

> . . . an ever-increasing process of industrialization which was resulting in a demand for labour, particularly skilled labour . . . There were simply not enough skilled workers to fill all the vacancies . . . with the result that increasing members of unskilled and semi-skilled workers, particularly blacks . . . had to be trained and utilized to perform higher-level skilled jobs.[7]

The percentage of whites in the labour force had dropped due to a drying-up of white immigrant labour. Whites in manufacturing dropped from 30% to 22.3%, and in construction from 25.4% to 13.9%.[8]

The report, in line with the economic realities it outlined, aimed at promoting the growth of a skilled black working class, and fitting them into the structure of apartheid's laws. In short, it aimed at eliminating some of the discrepancies within the apartheid labour system.

The most important "concession" the Wiehahn Report recommended was the recognition of black trade unions under the Industrial Conciliation Act of 1956, under which white unions are recognised. The press inside and outside South Africa greeted this as a truly major advance in South African industrial and racial relations. Mrs. Lucy Mvubelo, pro-government black trade unionist, told her critics South Africa had entered a new phase with rights and privileges being extended—although slowly—to black people . . ."I suggested to the (US) companies I visited that . . . they maintain investments in South Africa . . ."[9]

The Commission's reasons for recommending this move are interesting:

> The increasing opportunities for black workers to advance into job-categories previously occupied by non-blacks will soon give rise to the

anomalous situation where black workers working side by side with non-black workers in the same skilled occupations find themselves excluded from the statutory trade union system purely on the grounds of colour . . . Increased vertical labour mobility by job advancement through education and training, particularly of the black labour force, will place the statutory trade union system under extreme stress if the exclusion of the black worker from the system is perpetuated.[10]

In other words, the Wiehahn Commission wished to bring the skilled black worker into "the protective and stabilizing elements of the (Industrial Conciliation Act) system".[11]

The Wiehahn Commission did not recommend excluding migrant labour (primarily unskilled black labour) from trade union rights by law. But a closer reading of the Report shows that the Commissioners expected to exclude migrant labour from the trade unions by less explicit means.

On the one hand, it was felt that the migrants would not be interested: "It is unlikely that migrants would want to participate in union activities on any significant scale, and to pay membership dues".[12]

Since migrants take up their jobs on short-term contracts at fixed wages, it was suggested that the unions would have little to offer them. Further, "their low general level of education, their lack of experience of sophisticated labour relations systems" would make migrants "a largely alien and unassimilable presence in the unions".[13]

On the other hand, the structure of the Industrial Conciliation Act would in Wiehahn's view inhibit the unions themselves from attempting to organise migrant labourers. A union would be registered only if it managed to recruit a required proportion of eligible workers within the category it had defined for itself; if the union defined its membership to include migrants, who leave after a year, it would have to engage in a permanent recruiting drive to obtain the required proportion as members and thus retain its registration:

A union which set itself the herculean task of perpetually having to enlist transient workers would do so in the knowledge that it could achieve a sufficiently representative character only with immense difficulty, and never be free of the risk of losing its representativeness. Constitutional limitations are therefore likely to be imposed by unions themselves as a matter of pure self-interest.[14]

The Wiehahn Commission suggested directly that unions impose such self-limitations to keep out migrants:

The fear that unions would be dominated by migrants through sheer numbers cannot be regarded as realistic . . . It is unlikely in the extreme that unions would expose themselves to such possible domination if they had at their disposal simple means of preventing it—by requiring for example, that membership would be open to only persons who have worked a specified qualifying period (such as two years) within a particular industry, trade or occupation.[15]

Further, the extension of trade union rights to the skilled black working class is far from being seen as an unmixed blessing. Black trade unions, unregistered in terms of the Industrial Conciliation Act, have already achieved some undoubted successes. The twenty-seven unregistered black trade unions had a membership, according to Wiehahn, of between 50,000 and 70,000 workers in May 1978.[16]

The fact that their existence is not prohibited, while at the same time they are not registrable and are therefore excluded from the machinery of the Industrial Conciliation Act of 1956, serves as an incentive to foreign labour and political organisations to aid them overtly and covertly. Added to this is the fact that other non-labour organisations regard these unions as vehicles for change, using them also in matters other than those of a purely labour character.[17]

Being unregistered, black unions do not have to account for sources of income, whereas (white) registered unions do. Wiehahn commented:

Black trade unions are receiving large amounts of money from various sources, both internal and external . . . for example, during June 1978 two Black trade union federations received over R77,000 from overseas sources. These Black trade unions and other associated organisations are under no obligation to account for their income and expenditure, as is the case with registered trade unions, which in the opinion of the Commission is an undesirable state of affairs.[18]

Previously, black trade unions came under a 1977 amendment of the Black Labour Relations Regulations Act of 1953. By this amendment black "industrial negotiating committees" were set up between employers and employee groups, which could agree upon an informal "undertaking". A breach of such an "undertaking" was not subject to law, whereas a breach of an agreement reached in terms of the Industrial Conciliation Act of 1956 (recognising white unions) was a criminal offence.[19] Further:

One of the major objections to the Black Labour Relations Regulations (1953) was that committees were interpreted to be company unions set up in opposition to black trade unions".[20]

How effective such committees had been, the Report felt, was a moot point, since there was no record of what "undertakings" had been agreed upon. The unregistered black unions, on the other hand, had not felt too hampered by the presence of these "negotiating committees":

A significant number of enterprises have recognised unregistered black trade unions as bargaining partners, thus conferring upon some trade unions the privileges of recognition without the responsibility imposed by statute on non-black trade unions who do register.[21]

Thus the Wiehahn Commission believed that a separate process for evaluating black grievances, at least for the new skilled black working class, was not only discriminatory and unfair, but unsuccessful and possibly dangerous to industrial peace. It is fairly evident from the Report that it was felt black unskilled labour need not have any process at all for evaluating grievances.

On top of this, the Wiehahn Commission suggested several new measures to help control the new black unions registered under the Industrial Conciliation Act. Registration was to be at the discretion of the Industrial Registrar, in consultation with the National Manpower Commission, evaluating "a wide spectrum of considerations" and "weighing those applications . . . against the prevailing circumstances in the particular industry and against the implications for the country as a whole in the social, economic and political contexts".[22] Registration becomes not a right but a privilege.

The Commission recommended that the government extend the prohibition on political activities to all unions. Further, they suggested introducing a closer financial inspection of unions' funding. These measures will, of course, restrict white unions as well as black unions.

The Report did not suggest the government allow "mixed-race" unions: unions must remain either black or white.

Thus the extension of trade unions "rights" to Africans serves a double purpose. On the one hand, legal African trade unions could be expected to play a major role in helping to stabilize and strengthen the proposed skilled black working class, extending their privileges and ensuring their economic stability. On the other hand, this skilled black working class would be tied to and brought under the control of government institutions. They would not be allowed to develop into a force against the system.

The Wiehahn Report made two other recommendations calculated to help build a black skilled working class. First, they recommended the removal of job discrimination: all 28 categories of "trade reservation" should be eliminated. They noted: "Employer witnesses were uniformly in favour of abolition (of work reservation determinations), while (white) trade union witnesses were divided on the matter".[23]

Most job discrimination legislation has been ignored by employers and government for some time. The government has agreed, following the Wiehahn recommendations, to "phase out" such official discrimination, following negotiations with the white unions involved. Unofficial and informal discrimination remains.

Secondly, they suggested adjusting the law to allow in-service training, technical schools, and other industry-related education for Africans, also to permit African apprentices in "white areas", previously forbidden by law.

The Wiehahn Commission also recommended the formation of a National Manpower Commission to oversee all labour-related issues and report on them, and to help make the economy more efficient, under the control of the Department of Labour (now Manpower Utilization). This Commission should also be linked to the Ministry of Defence, to avoid duplication on questions of industrial and defence manpower needs.

Altogether, the Wiehahn Commission made the promotion of a black skilled working class part of the new government policy, not to destroy apartheid but to preserve it.

The government did not, however, accept the Wiehahn Report whole-heartedly. The Minister of Manpower Utilization, Fanie Botha, has claimed that by mid-1980 the recommendations of the report will be "enshrined in legislation"[24] but some measures have been welcomed more enthusiastically and implemented more rapidly than others.

Section 77 of the Industrial Conciliation Act, the section upholding job reservation, has been cancelled. By the time it had been legally removed, 23 job "determinations" had already been eliminated, with only five remaining. These five the government promised to phase out in concert with the white unions; the legislation eliminating Section 77 made substantive provision for their temporary retention.[25]

The Government accepted the Wiehahn recommendation that apprenticeship be open to all races in principle. But they made no provisions in the law to advance this principle. Likewise, the integration of racially segregated facilities in factories and in offices, while in principle accepted by government, has not yet been made law. The state has, in line with the Wiehahn recommendations, created a National Manpower Commission and restructured the Industrial Tribunal as an Industrial Court empowered to adjudicate disputes of rights and create a body of case law.[26]

The government's main point of difference with the Wiehahn Report came over the question of trade union rights for black workers. The White Paper accepting most of the Report explicitly provided barriers to keep migrant labour out of the trade unions: only permanent residents in fixed, not contract, employment would be allowed union membership (although exemptions might be considered in special cases). Black unions would be registered provisionally: full registration would follow later. African unions would have to show themselves acceptable to the State before registration would be permitted. The Government then reinforced this as a means of controlling the new black unions by "strongly discouraging the non-registered black unions", cancelling any "informal" agreements already signed between them and the employers, prohibiting collection of dues. The Government's attitude was summarized by Mr. S. P. Botha, Minister of Manpower Utilization (Labour):

> "What we are doing now is we are allowing black trade unions to be registered, which in effect means that once they are registered they will be under the discipline of the Industrial Conciliation Act. That's what it boils down to . . ."[27]

The government White Paper was immediately attacked both inside and outside South Africa, for excluding migrants and "homelanders" from trade union rights. As one *Sunday Post* article emphasised:

> "Labour experts I spoke to this week said the black workers movement faced a serious crisis if enough black unions take up the government's tempting offer to register, thereby entering into a state and industry controlled bargaining system. Thousands—perhaps even millions— of

black workers would be permanently excluded from negotiating on the fruits of their labour.

This would mean, they said, the creation of a serious split between the interests of urban workers and those of rural and home-based workers".[28]

Most of the independent black trade unions have stated that they would only register on their own terms. It is clear that this much-publicized concession was intended to bring the black union movement under greater government control.

In reaction, the government reversed its stand on migrants and bantustan residents, stating that they too could be exempted from the ban on trade union membership. (Perhaps like the Wiehahn Commission the government also believes this "right" will go unused.) Workers from foreign countries and persons who "entered the Republic temporarily to undertake specific tasks and then return to their countries" (i.e. alien contract workers) would remain excluded.[29]

However, this new dispensation failed to satisfy the black trade unions completely. First, some doubts remained as to the sincerity of the new measures. The Western Province General Workers' Union, with a membership that is 80% migrant labour, pointed out that this move "could simply mean that unions have to police themselves . . . The Wiehahn Commission implied that unions with a small migrant membership would find it easier to register. We fear that unions may have to limit the extent of migrant membership to gain registration".[30] Further, migrants' trade union "rights" had been established by Ministerial proclamation, not by law, and could be removed by the same simple process.

More significantly, black unionists objected to the whole pattern of control that registration would impose. The 50,000 strong Federation of South African Trade Unions (FOSATU) published the following conditions upon which it would consider registration: that unions must be non-racial in their membership and control; that provisional registration, which involves "rights" that may be removed at the end of a trial period, would be unacceptable; that additional controls (such as financial investigation) would not be acceptable; and that the existing unions must be registered as of right, not as a privilege, as they now stand.[31] As of November 1979, 17 black trade unions had refused to register under the Industrial Conciliation Act (three Cape unions and 14 FOSATU members).[32]

This situation is clearly not stable. The registered white unions have begun to demand compulsory registration of the unregistered black unions, and the government is considering such action: "Confederation of Labour men argue that it is essential that registration be made compulsory so that black unions can be subjected to the control we were promised."[33]

Other measures already initiated, such as cancelling agreements between employers and unregistered unions, may force black unions to consider registration. Indeed, the *Financial Mail* has predicted that it is possible that:

... the issue will become not one of whether black unions are prepared to register, but whether they are allowed to. The registrar will have wide new powers and it is unlikely that he will allow all the existing unregistered unions into the new system ...

Most sources believe a 'weeding-out' process will take place in which the authorities will decide which presently unregistered unions are acceptable. And the more militant unions, they argue, are unlikely to get in. They could be out of business.[34]

Perhaps the best summary of the impact of the Wiehahn Report comes in a National Party pamphlet distributed during the Randfontein by-election. This dispelled any lingering doubts one might have about the Report's intentions.

Wiehahn Report

(is) to the advantage of all South Africa BECAUSE:
—the creation of more skilled job opportunities increases the growth rate.
—an increased growth rate gives South Africa an economic power base in the military struggle for survival.
—labour unrest will be restricted to the minimum.
—the abolition of statutory work reservation will stimulate the influx of foreign capital ... Since it became known that the government accepted the recommendations of the Wiehahn Report in principle, more than R500,000,000 has entered the country ...
—the position of the white worker among others will be protected more efficiently—statutory work reservation protected only one out of every 200 white workers ...

27 black trade unions *which exist already* and have a membership of some 70,000 are now being effectively brought under the discipline and control of the law.

This includes:
—a ban on political activities
—control over their membership
—access to their constitutions
—access to their financial statements and balance sheets
—control over their funds by a State Inspector ...

It is not true ...
that white workers will have to make way for blacks.
It is not true ...
that whites and non-whites will, necessarily, have to share facilities.
Make sure of the facts and vote National on June the 6th for the sake of Progress and Stability.[35]

So, under closer examination, most of the much advertised "concessions" made by the government add up to the creation of privilege for the small number of rich or professional urban Africans. They can buy houses, they can eat in restaurants, they can operate businesses more freely. To a lesser extent the government seems committed to building up a skilled black working class as well, offering them trade union privileges, industrial training, and so on. Other "changes" merely preserve the same institutions in a new form or behind a black face—the community councils, black education, sports policies.

Behind all these changes the white bureacracy gains larger and larger discretionary powers. Thus, as the *Financial Mail* commented:

A person disqualified by parliament on racial grounds may suddenly aquire rights and privileges at the whim of an official, who is a law unto himself. Yet another disqualified person may be refused or denied the same privilege.[36]

The "concessions" have not led to any significant change:

... Plastering discriminatory laws with exemptions is not the answer. The exemptions are at best a face-saving palliative. The only valid solution is the removal of apartheid laws ... Wriggle, exempt and concede as it will, the government will not get off the apartheid hook until it takes the only step that counts—and that is to scourge racial discrimination from the Statute Book.[37]

Part Two: Repression

On 8 November [*1979*] the Prime Minister said that a
reckless or careless Government could turn South Africa
into a powderkeg within a matter of days . . . we are now
watching the fuse to that powderkeg burn shorter by the
day.[1]

Black Sash Emergency Report

The creation of a privileged stratum of Africans, however, has an unavoidable
corollary: the rest of the African population must be even more firmly controlled. If the government merely aims at creating a small black middle class to
support it against the unruly majority—as has been their stated intention—
then that majority faces more stringent repression. And to the extent that big
business and government turn towards mechanization and the creation of a
skilled black working class, there will be increasing black unemployment, with
resulting hardship and discontent.

This indeed has been the other side of the coin of Botha's changes. Owing to
the impact of the world recession, unemployment has risen disastrously for the
black population in South Africa. The Department of Statistics officially claims
9% of economically active Africans are unemployed (501,000 people); the
Minister of Manpower Utilization Fanie Botha puts the figure of total unemployment at "over a million" people, of whom most are African.[2] Independent
researchers put African unemployment as high as 25%, rising to 27-30% by
1990.[3] Hand in hand with this, the government has cracked down on the
unemployed.

RESIDENCE

Tighter Influx Control
First, the government has tightened up the enforcement of the numerous
apartheid laws that control the "economically unproductive". In April 1978 the
government began a wave of "crime prevention blitzes". Police and army, with
guns and fixed bayonets, cordoned off Soweto and Alexandra (on 1 April) and
Hillbrow (on 15 April). People entering and leaving the area were searched
indiscriminately, ostensibly for "criminals":

> The sweep, described by Col. Gert Slabbert, head of the Johannesburg
> Riot Squad, as "a routine operation" was also designed to pioneer combined

operations between army, police and traffic officers . . . The army will be called in on all future operations to assist police in combating many offences.[4]

The Hillbrow sweep, ostensibly following the (apolitical) murder of two white schoolboys, included 1,000 policemen in house-to-house searches, with 1,600 arrests—not, ironically, including the murderer. It was under the leadership of Brigadier Theuns Swanepoel, notorious in political cases as a torturer. The Divisional Commissioner of Police for the Witwatersrand said: "One can describe the massive police action as a show of force".[5]

In the following months, these massive "crime crackdowns" continued and spread. Any doubt about their role as a population control measure was stifled when the then Minister of Justice Mr. Kruger admitted in Parliament that over 95% of the 3,080 arrested in these operations were arrested for pass, curfew and trespass offences.[6] Approximate figures for "crime crackdown" arrests had reached over 5,000 by Mid-May. And they continued, becoming a nearly daily occurrence by June, to the extent that an article summarizing arrests in the week ending 14 June mentioned several raids not reported elsewhere, with about 1,000 arrests: the swoops no longer counted as newsworthy. Further, the police frequently refused to announce the numbers of those arrested.[7]

The number of Africans arrested for pass offences in 1978 increased by 36% over the year before—272,887 in 1978 compared to 173,571 in 1977. The main reasons given for the increase were "anti-crime sweeps" and bantustan unemployment (forcing people illegally into the cities to hunt for jobs).[8]

In February of 1979 it was revealed that pass arrests in Johannesburg had doubled over the rate at the end of 1978. 4,084 people appeared in Johannesburg courts on pass offences between 15-31 January 1979, twice as many as in November 1978, four times as many as in December 1978.[9] A *Sunday Express* expose on Johannesburg pass courts revealed that cases were "tried" in 40 seconds to 3 minutes each, depending upon the magistrate: fines ran from R15 to R30 or 60 days; people without the correct papers but legally in the area were remanded in jail for a week for "investigation".[10] In 1979 altogether 120,000 people were arrested by the South African police on pass law "offences", according to official figures.[11]

Crossroads

In moves which are part-and-parcel of influx control, the government has also moved drastically against the pockets of illegal housing, where people stay who are not qualified to live in the urban areas, or who for other reasons (such as the housing shortage) have been unable to find legal accommodation.

The most dramatic case comes with the squatter townships around Cape Town. The government has for some time spent a lot of energy trying to prevent the immigration of Africans to Cape Town, claiming that there should be no "indigenous" African population in the Western Cape, only white and Coloured people. All Africans must enter the Cape as migrant "contract" labour. This policy, not surprisingly, is widely ignored by Africans, and large squatter townships have grown up on the flats around the city to house the thousands of "illegal immigrants", mostly men legally employed but illegally resident, with their equally illegal wives and families.

In August 1977, the government bulldozed Modderdam shanty town near Cape Town, leaving 26,000 people homeless. Many of them however, either stayed in the area or returned to it after a brief period: Modderdam was replaced by other shanty-towns. In January, 1978, 10,000 people were evicted from Unibell squatter township.

In July 1978 the government announced that it would move on a third squatter town, Crossroads, in September. The residents, with the backing of the churches and the white liberal community, announced they would resist. On 7 September, the police cordoned off Crossroads at midnight and conducted house-to-house pass checks.[12] When they attempted to repeat the pass raid a week later, they were met by a crowd: police beat the squatters with sticks, used teargas, and fired guns. Two Africans were shot dead and possibly a baby was trampled to death (sources disagree); another 14 squatters were treated in hospital; 10 policemen were injured by the stoning; 300 people were arrested for "pass offences", and four Africans disappeared, presumed detained.[13] Of those arrested a number were not allowed bail. Squatter leader Johnson Nxobongwana was severely beaten by police and hospitalized.[14] The then Deputy Minister of Plural Relations Mr. Vosloo reaffirmed that Crossroads would be removed before the end of the year: "people who refuse to leave will be 'carried away' or removed by even harsher methods", he said.[15]

Not only did the residents of Crossroads resist, but they gained massive support throughout the world. The government hesitated to destroy the township outright. In early October, however, the press revealed that South Africa had secretly begun to construct a "large emergency township" (or resettlement camp) on the Kei river near Queenstown for Crossroads residents. The land had been "expropriated by the South African Bantu Trust for eventual incorporation into the Transkei", and so the Transkei would be forced to accept the "removed" Crossroads population against its will.[16]

The Transkei protested; the government backed down. The new Minister of Cooperation and Development, Dr Piet Koornhof, announced a reprieve for Crossroads in April 1979. Crossroads would be replaced by a "model township" in Cape Town of 1860 "dignified and acceptable family housing units"— although later it was announced that "no more than two families would be allowed to live in each of the houses".[17] Those residents with Section 10 rights (permitted to live permanently in the urban area with their families), contract workers in full employment and their dependants (a group not normally permitted housing in the Cape) and other families "deserving special consideration" would be housed; persons without legal means of support would be removed.[18] Crossroads residents calculated that nearly all the township inhabitants were in the former categories. One survey by Maree and Cornell in 1978 revealed that, of the 288 Crossroads households they surveyed, 50% of the household heads were legally in the area for an average of 18.2 years; 81% of the household heads were employed in the formal sector; 11.2% were (legally) employed in the informal sector; only 6% were unemployed (and therefore would be removed). Another survey, by Weichell and Graaf (in 1978) found that of 902 men surveyed, 98% had been employed in Cape Town since 1975, and 81% since 1970.[19]

Individual Crossroads residents who qualified for the new housing were however still subjected to the risk of being "endorsed out" by police. So in July the government agreed to offer temporary six-month residence permits to Crossroads residents who were to be rehoused. Thus residents reacted with shock when Dr. G. de V. Morrison, Deputy Minister for Cooperation and Development, announced that some 3,000 families "living illegally in Crossroads" would after all be resettled in the homelands.[20]

It turned out that the over 90 per cent of Crossroads population engaged in legal employment in Cape Town were not by any means all "legally" employed: many were employed while illegally resident in the area and therefore never registered as employed (which would expose their illegal residence status, even though the job itself was perfectly legal). The "temporary residence permits" specifically did not enable employers to register their unregistered employees, no matter how long they had been employed. Recommendations following the Riekert Commission Report introduced a R500 fine for the employer caught employing an unregistered worker (*see below*): the result was that such workers would be sacked. (As we shall see below, the "moratorium" on this fine did not apply to the Western Cape. The temporary residence permits did exempt employers from the R500 fine for the six months they covered, so that such workers were not all sacked at once; but since workers carrying such permits could not be registered, this merely deferred the day when they would be fired.)

The effect of Dr. Koornhof's confusing and delaying tactics was recorded in the *Guardian*:

> Six months have now passed, and critics of apartheid have turned their backs on this community and sought out new issues with which to embarrass the Government, but it now seems that three-quarters of the families in Crossroads are about to be evicted from their homes and deposited in the poverty-stricken homelands. Koornhof is apparently confident that he can inflict this fate with impunity.[21]

Other Removals

Crossroads is the most dramatic example of threatened removal—it is far from the only one. A major series of removals took place in late 1978 with the mass evictions of 250,000 to 300,000 non-Tswana residents in BophuthaTswana.[22] This also provided a new twist to race classification; that people from one "language group" could be evicted from a bantustan to which they did not officially belong, even if they had been removed to that bantustan by the South

African government in the first instance. Police began to raid squatters in the Winterveldt area near Pretoria for passes in July 1978. In November, Bophuta-Tswana's Prime Minister warned that more than 12,000 Ndebeles must leave BophuthaTswana or take out BophuthaTswana citizenship before February.[23] On 3 December 1978 30,000 people in the Klipgat area were given 15 days to move, but no place to move to. BophuthaTswana citizenship was not considered a mitigating factor in this case. Within 15 days all 30,000 people appeared to have "vanished" in compliance with the eviction orders, presumably to other squatter towns.[24] Another non-Tswana community, at Stinkwater, were told they must leave despite the fact that they claimed they were removed to that place by the South African government in 1965.[25] There has been no organized resistance to these removals, and no consistent publication of the plight of these people.

In Thaba Nchu, in the Orange Free State, part of BophutaTswana, squatters classified as "South Sotho" resisted eviction to a temporary resettlement camp 13 miles away, in April 1978. Three hundred were arrested and one woman was shot dead.[26] In August 1978, several hundred squatter shacks in Duncan Village, East London, were burnt down by the government, following police raids and hundreds of arrests. Forty thousand Africans are due to be removed from this area to make way for Indian and Coloured Group Areas; the Indians and Coloureds, however, have so far refused to take the land that has been cleared for them in this way.[27]

In October 1978 officials denied that shacks in Parkside, East London had been "indiscriminately razed". They claimed rather that:

> Raids, arrests and burning of shacks took place in the past week in the Buffalo and Parkside flats areas. The spokesman said board officials had conducted raids mainly on shacks built with cardboard cartons. The shacks were considered a health hazard.[28]

Eliminating this "health hazard" left two to three hundred people homeless.[29]

In Durban, 500 squatter families in Clermont faced demolition in November 1978. Their homes were temporarily saved by intervention by Black Sash officials, the Diakonia church organisation and Clermont Ratepayers' Association; but on 2 December, the demolitions were resumed "despite Government assurances that action would be halted until further investigation".[30]

In March 1979, the government admitted that 42,000 people in the Upper Tugela region were scheduled for removal to an area "between Drakensberg locations 1 and 2, and certain farms adjacent to Drakensberg location number 1"; the people had not yet been informed of these impending removals since negotiations with tribal authorities were still in progress.[31] In May, Zulu leaders and government agreed to remove some 3,000 of these people to the Oliviershoek area.[32] Twenty thousand families from Sibongile, Tembalihle and Bhekuzu in Northern Natal are also to be removed to Nqutu and Mondlo in KwaZulu.[33]

In Alexandra, Johannesburg, people danced in the streets in February 1979 following an announcement by Dr. Koornhof that the township would not be

removed to be replaced entirely by single-sex hostels.[34] However, in July it came
to light that 622 Coloured families would still be resettled in Klipspruit West.[35]

120 families from the Sinthumule and Kutama areas of Venda have been
removed to Indermark, west of Pietersburg; another 800 families are due to
follow. Indermark is 17 miles from the nearest shop, and has no health facilities,
and only two temporary schools.[36]

There have been too many mass evictions and removals to include all cases
here—and many do not reach the press at all. But even this partial list can leave
no doubt that the new "verligte" government has not greatly mitigated the
system of uprooting people implicit in the territorial separation that is Grand
Apartheid.

Group Areas Act Prosecutions

The government also began in 1979 to enforce the Group Areas Act more
thoroughly against Indians and Coloureds. Before this richer Indian and
Coloured families could and did live illegally in white areas such as Hillbrow
(with the consent of their landlords; these are not shantytowns by any means).
Since there has never been enough housing in their own "designated areas", the
government previously winked at this infringement. However, in February
1979 over 250 people appeared in Johannesburg courts for illegally living in
white areas: "the number is growing daily so much so that the courts will have
difficulty getting through all the cases".[37]

The press revealed a right-wing campaign (by the National Front) to search
out Coloureds and Indians living in white areas and report them to the police.
This reputedly caused the police crackdown.[38] Far from easing up on residential
control, therefore, the Botha government has imposed it even more rigidly.

Bantustan policy

The government has accompanied this tightening up of existing regulations by a
strengthening of its stand on the bantustans.

A third bantustan, the Venda bantustan, was forced into independence on
13 September 1979. The "elections" preceding the decision for independence
are worthy of note. The Venda opposition party (the Venda Independence
Party) in July 1978 won a majority of the elected seats—31 out of 42—in the
Venda Legislative Assembly; however, Chief Mphephu remained the leader of
the Assembly by virtue of the remaining elected seats plus 42 "designated
chiefs and headmen" who also sit in the Assembly. In August Chief Mphephu
detained 37 prominent Venda citizens, including nine opposition members of
the Legislative Assembly and three magistrates. The newspapers reported that
"criminal proceedings . . . would follow investigations by South African police
operating in the territory". By 29 August 11 out of the 42 elected members were
detained.[39] The other opposition members, meeting in Soweto, voted to boycott
the legislative assembly; in September 1978, with 12 opposition members
detained and the rest boycotting the assembly, Chief Mphephu was re-elected

without a dissenting vote.[40] The *Post* editorial of 12 September called this "the final nail in the coffin of separate development's credibility", and went on to ask:

> Are we to assume that Dr. Mulder will now go ahead and negotiate with Chief Mphephu about the independence of Venda, in spite of the evidence that the former does not represent the wishes of the people of the homeland?[41]

This is precisely what Dr. Mulder's successor Dr. Piet Koornhof did, and Venda has now joined BophutaTswana and the Transkei as an "independent nation".

And the government plans to go ahead with its schedule of homeland independence. In November 1979, Prime Minister Botha suggested a "homeland consolidation programme" to make them more credible as separate nations, at a projected cost of R3,000 millions.[42] The 1979 budget, however, only allotted some R69 millions for homeland consolidation.[43] Whether government will come up with the sums required is perhaps questionable.

Citizenship

Government policy states that there will eventually be no black South African citizens. All Africans will be citizens of independent bantustans instead. In line with this, the government has redefined the category of "homeland citizen" to even further encroach upon the rights of urban Africans. In January 1978 the Bantu Affairs Department announced that all children born after 26 March 1970, were automatically bantustan citizens irrespective of the status of their parents. They thus automatically lost their urban rights, except as dependants of urban residents; upon reaching their majority they would be "repatriated" to their "homeland" if they are unemployed—even if they were born and bred in the urban area.[44]

A year later, the citizenship position was refined once more. People born in urban areas *before* 1970 previously qualified for the coveted "section 10 rights" enabling them to live permanently within white areas. In January 1979, the Botha government did away with this too: "The birthplace of an applicant would no longer be used as a criteria for a pass". Although influx control requirements would "remain the same" in theory, a person born in a white area would be counted as a citizen of the "homeland" of his parent's "tribe," no matter what his date of birth. If his "homeland" was independent, the person would lose South African citizenship, and with it any rights he may have to stay in "white" South Africa.[45] To quote the Witwatersrand Chief Commissioner in the Department of Plural Relations:

> Whereas in the past people born and bred in Johannesburg were assured of getting a reference book, this will not be the case anymore.[46]

The "Idle Bantu" Law

Besides enforcing existing laws to implement influx control, the government has instituted new measures to strengthen it. The first such measure was known as

51

the "Idle Bantu Bill", pushed through Parliament in the January 1979 session. The law, section 29 of the Black (Urban Areas) Consolidation Act, amends the definition of "idle", which previously referred to a person "normally unemployed", to include any African who is:

> ... not lawfully employed and has for a period or periods in the aggregate of not less than 122 days during the preceding 12 months not been lawfully employed.[47]

Any African unemployed for more than four months in the year, and not necessarily four consecutive months, can be picked up and brought before a Commissioner (within 72 hours of arrest). The Commissioner decides if the person is "idle" in the above terms. If he is declared "idle", the African loses his Section 10(1) (a) or (b) rights (his permission to stay in the urban area) and all the benefits that go with it (for instance, the right to occupy a house he owns under the 99-year-leasehold). Further, the Commissioner may order any African so declared to be removed from the area: to be settled in a rural village or other settlement, or to be detained for up to two years on a farm colony, refuge or rescue home.[48]

When the "Idle Bantu Bill" first came before Parliament government critics pointed out that it would penalize a man who was unemployed through no fault of his own and was genuinely seeking work. The Minister of Plural Relations and Development then claimed that he would exempt from the 122-day provision any person who was registered as a workseeker and had not been offered lawful employment in the preceding 122 days. Dr. Koornhof also assured parliament that a workseeker could turn down such employment if he wished without making himself vulnerable to the law's provisions.

However, the Institute of Race Relations points out:

> A close scrutiny of the existing act shows, however, that persons who are registered as workseekers may still be declared "idle".[49]

Also, the law states a person may be declared "idle" if he "without lawful cause refuses suitable employment"—and the definition of "suitable" is left very vague. The new amendment retains its original force: Africans unemployed for the requisite four months, for whatever the reason, can still be defined as "idle".

The "Idle Bantu" amendment was passed and is now law. However, the very harshness of its provisions has ironically prevented it from being used as frequently as at least some sections of government would like. The Riekert Commission of Inquiry reported complaints from some witnesses giving evidence to it that, since the law provided up to two years of confinement or forced labour (on a farm colony), appeal courts often refused to uphold the original conviction:

> the review courts adopted "an almost humanist attitude" and in cases of a first finding that a person was idle or undesirable, often suspend the execution of a warrant...[50]

The "Idle Bantu" clause may have been ineffective: it is still on the books. Other changes to enforce influx control however may well prove more efficient.

THE URBAN ORDER

The Riekert Commission Report

The main government attempt to strengthen influx control has been through the Riekert Commission of Inquiry into Legislation affecting the Utilization of Manpower (excluding the legislation administered by the Departments of Labour or Mines). This Report examined the whole complex body of legislation referring to "manpower" (meaning Africans and influx control) in order to eliminate " outdated or unnecessary statutory provisions as well as administrative rules"; to eliminate "all inconsistencies in existing legislation, regulation and administrative rules"; to spell out provisions clearly "to make possible their uniform applications"; in effect, to simplify and streamline the laws relating to influx control to make them work better. The report was released on 9 May 1979.[1]

Dr. Riekert is Economic Adviser to the Prime Minister and the solitary member of the Commission of Inquiry. He specifically stated his frame of reference as follows:

> The policy of the present government in this connection (*influx control*) was put as follows (*by the then Minister of Bantu Administration*) . . . in 1972 . . . "The first and most fundamental point of policy is . . . that every black person in South Africa, wherever he may find himself, is a member of his specific nation . . ." "The second . . . The Bantu in the white area, whether they were born here or whether they were allowed to come here under our control laws, are here for the labour they are being allowed to perform. The third principle . . . is that the fundamental citizenship rights may only be enjoyed by a Bantu person within his own ethnic homeland . . ." "The fourth policy point . . . is that the maximum number of people must be present in their own homeland".[2]

These are the basic rules of apartheid and they are the principles his report embodies; these are the measures he hoped to render "simplified and streamlined".

The method envisioned by Commissioner Riekert to thus preserve and extend apartheid involved concentrating on two basic points of control: jobs and housing. As he explained:

> Controlled employment and controlled accommodation are the two pillars on which the ordering of the urbanization process and sound and orderly community development ought to rest".[3]

Or, to put it more bluntly, the aim was

> . . . more effective control over migration than in the past, and the avoidance of much of the friction that accompanied such control in the past, in that emphasis will be placed mainly on the *control of employment and control of accommodation*[4] (*original emphasis*).

In theory, both of these points were regulated already by the apartheid laws. Riekert proposed to make this control as absolute as possible.

The previous regulations covering black employment, in the Black (Bantu) Labour Act of 1964, set up a system of labour bureaux. The function of these was to place Africans in employment and regulate the supply of labour, especially from the bantustans. Instead of a system in which the labourer offered to sell his labour on a "free market", the bantustan African went to the labour bureau which offered him what was usually his only chance of legally finding work on a contract to an urban area for a specified period of time (usually one year). Some employers directly hired Africans from the rural areas as well. But in law, at least, employers were supposed to register all job vacancies with the labour bureaux, and further register all new employees as those vacancies filled. This would enable the labour bureaux to keep the Reference Bureaux informed of African workers, and to collect data on the structure of the job market.

This system proved very cumbersome: "In practice, many employers fail to fulfil these obligations".[5] The labour bureaux were inefficient bureaucracies, and the penalties for failing to register were mild for the employer (if not mild for the African worker, who was permanently in danger of being "endorsed out" if caught). Indeed, ". . . some employers preferred to make use of the services of African workers who were unlawfully in the area . . ."[6] An unregistered employee found himself in no position to protest against low wages or bad conditions.

In a survey in 1978, Dr. Lied Loots found that only 4.5% of the urban men surveyed had found their jobs through the labour bureaux system and only 0.5% of the rural men had done so. Urban men found their employment through door-to-door canvassing (35.9%); through family or friends (29.2%); by recommendation or transfer from a previous employer (16.9%); and through application by letter (13.7%). Rural men found their jobs through door-to-door canvassing (36.6%); through family and friends (25.9%); by letter (21%) and through past employers (16.2%).[7] The labour bureaux clearly were not an efficient means of controlling the supply of African labour.

The Riekert Report suggested strengthening this system of labour bureaux in two ways to make it an effective means of control. First, "The attestation of contracts of employment should be strictly enforced in all cases at the place of recruitment".[8] It was argued that

Contracts of employment ensured identification and control, obviated misunderstandings, afforded protection to employers and employees, and recognized the authority of the governments of Black States over their citizens.[9]

That the contract be registered at the place of recruitment was equally crucial for control: it would mean that an African illegally present in an urban area could not find a job there, because he could not be registered as an employee without revealing his illegal status. Unlike the previous system of registration, where there was little or no attempt to co-ordinate job registration with the legal position of the worker, the Riekert system would make the first

54

dependent upon the second. Thus, the Report argued, "illegals" in urban areas would eventually disappear, because they had no hope of finding employment. It was also recommended that legally attested contracts should not exceed one year in length—thus ensuring a check on the labourer at least once every year, and that the labourer remained a migrant.

Secondly, the Riekert Report proposed introducing much more severe penalties against employers who fail to register their workers: "The only way to bring unlawful employment to an end is to take much stricter action against employers in future".[10] The unemployed African, it was pointed out, stood only to gain by seeking illegal employment if such employment were available: an illegal job was a greater attraction than the legal deterrents.

In a study published in October 1979, it was concluded that a worker from a bantustan stood to gain financially from illegally holding a job even if he spent nine months out of the year in jail (and thus without an income). The table below shows the percentage that a worker's income increased if he moved from a rural to an urban area, and how that percentage was affected if he spent a period in jail for illegal residence in that urban area. For example, a worker who moves from the Ciskei to Pietermaritzburg earns seven times his previous income—even if he spends 3 months out of the year in jail.

	Ciskei/ Pietermaritz- burg	Lebowa/ Johannes- burg	Bophutha- Tswana/ Pretoria
Nine months work/ three months jail	702.7%	255.0%	85.4%
Six months work/ six months jail	468.5%	170.0%	56.9%
Three months work/ nine months jail	234.2%	85.0%	28.5%

(from *Financial Mail 12.10.79*)

By putting the burden of the penalties upon the employer, these job possibilities would disappear—and so would the "illegals" in urban areas.

According to Riekert this tightening of the laws regulating contracts of employment would necessarily be accompanied by an over-haul of the labour bureaux themselves. No individual employers could recruit for themselves: they would have to requisition the number of workers they wanted from the labour bureaux. However, employers' groups would be allowed and even encouraged to recruit in concert with the labour bureaux (the prime case being the mine recruiting organizations). The labour bureaux themselves would have to be improved, as the Government later recommended:

A programme of action should be initiated to ensure the efficient functioning of the labour bureaux system and particular emphasis should be laid on the improvement of the quality of the services rendered, the training of the labour bureau staff, and the establishment of separate service points for different categories of workers, for example for professional and clerical workers and for unskilled workers.[11]

The rural African, in this revised system, would have no choice but to become a migrant labourer, offered a contract to fulfil a requisition by an employer in the prescribed (white) area, sent to that area for no more than a year, and sent home at the end of that period.

To control accommodation, Riekert also proposed to build upon the existing apartheid structure. The Report endorsed the "Section 10" rights which give some Africans permission to remain permanently in an urban area. At the same time it advocated reinforcing the system by which people without Section 10(1) (a), (b) or (c) rights can only get accommodation in an urban area if they have a job which, as we saw above, is to be tied firmly to the migrant labour system:

> In order to regulate the movement of labour from rural areas to urban areas and from black states or independent states to white rural areas, it will be necessary to include in the proposed "Employment and Training Act" a provision for control of residence . . . (and) a provision . . . that no employment may take place without the authorization of the labour bureau concerned. In this connection, a distinction must be drawn between established workers within the jurisdiction of the labour bureau concerned and the workers moving to that area. In the case of the former a standing authorization should be granted enabling the worker concerned to change employers within the area concerned without further authorization from the labour bureau . . . In the case of the latter group of workers, the authorization of the labour bureau, must, in addition to any requirements in respect of the attestation of contracts of employment and the authorization from the government concerned for the worker to leave that government's area, be subject to:—
>
> (i) A firm offer of employment
> (ii) the non-availability of suitable local workseekers; and
> (iii) the availability of approved housing.[12]

Tying the possibility of employment to the availability of housing controls influx in two ways. On the one hand, government can regulate the rate of influx by controlling the number of houses and beds available in overall terms by building or restricting the building of new houses and hostels. While government can not, in theory at least, control the number of new houses built by township owners under the 99-year leasehold and home ownership schemes, it can control the number of sites available. Also such housing is open only to those who already have Section 10(1) (a) and (b) rights. All other houses have to be funded by government through administration boards (or eventually the community councils). On the other hand, the employer can (and often at present does) reserve blocks of hostel beds and sometimes houses with the local administration board for the use of his migrant labour. The individual migrant or "homelander" arriving in the city would only be able to get accommodation if he has already signed a contract before his arrival: there would be no other

56

options available. An African arriving illegally in an urban area would be forced out because (1) he could not get accommodation, which would be tied to his having a job; and (2) he could not get a job, which would be dependent upon his having legal accommodation already.

People who already possess Section 10(1) (a), (b) or (c) rights, of course, would not be particularly affected by this dilemma. They would already have approved accommodation in the urban area, since these rights specifically "enable blacks to become eligible for the allotment of family housing".[13]

The Riekert Report assumed people with Section 10(1) (a), (b) and (c) qualifications would become a new elite. Such rights, it pointed out:

(a) Freed blacks from the restrictive provision that they could not be in a prescribed area for longer than 72 hours; (b) afforded security against removal from a prescribed area; (c) enabled blacks to become eligible for the allotment of family housing; (d) enabled a black person buying or erecting his own house to bring his family from elsewhere to join him; (e) accorded preference in so far as the admission of children to schools was concerned; (f) enabled a black person to apply for the issue of a trading licence or to set up as an independent contractor; (g) enabled a black person to take part in the election of community councils and to make himself available for election to such a council; (h) enabled the children of a black person to obtain section 10(1) (a) qualifications and (i) accorded preference in the allocation of employment and afforded protection against competition from workers not having such qualifications.[14]

Riekert suggested further concessions to the privileged urban African. It recommended that men with these qualifications who marry women from rural areas be allowed to "import" them into the urban areas, which was previously prohibited. It recommended the elimination of all restrictions on African businessmen, at least in the black areas. It suggested strengthening the community councils, and giving them more local authority. And it suggested that Section 10 rights become transferable from one urban area to another, depending again upon the availability of housing:

The provisions of Section 10(1) (a) and (b) of the Act have a restrictive effect on inter-urban and intra-urban mobility of black workers . . . and are not conducive to the optimal utilization of the present black manpower in the white area of South Africa.[15]

In effect, this would mean an African with Section 10 rights could move from one job to another with the urban areas, or be transferred by the same employer from one area to another without losing these rights.

Riekert also proposed that people with Section 10(1) (a), (b) and (c) rights should not have to have their documents endorsed each time they changed jobs, although their employers would have to observe the "normal registration procedure" (thus keeping their movements on central records). The urban African himself need only apply once for a standing authorization to work in the urban areas.

Lastly, the Commission emphasized that urban Africans should be given preference over rural migrants for jobs. It was recognized that this would not necessarily meet the approval of employers:

> . . . preference was given by many employers to contract workers from black states . . .
> (a) The employer was aware of the fact that a section 10 1 (a) worker enjoyed a reasonable degree of permanency in the area, and that, if he left the employer's service, he could easily find other employment. As against this, the section 10(1) (d) worker did not enjoy a similar opportunity and therefore tended to stick to his job because usually he would have to return to his home area when he left the employ of the employer concerned. Consequently in many cases employers preferred a worker who had to obtain a section 10(1) (d) concession.
> (b) The black worker who was imported from a black state was usually prepared to offer his services at a lower price than the section 10(1) (a) worker, causing many employers to prefer employing a section 10(1) (d) worker.[16]

Nevertheless, it was felt that urban Africans should have priority for jobs in urban areas, since they were already resident there. This would limit the number of migrants even on a one-year contract to the minimum necessary. Commissioner Riekert commented:

> It is a question of how to divide the limited job opportunities available . . . We give priority to urban blacks because they at least have houses. If people were allowed to flow into the cities irrespective of the demand for labour, slums would result and wages be undercut.
> . . . Unemployment is an overall problem not caused by my Commission.
> . . . The idea of giving welfare aid is out of my terrain.[17]

The Report was not concerned with the social effects of rural unemployment. On the other hand, urban unemployment was to be discouraged. The urban elite tended, in the Commission's opinion, to get out of hand:

> The majority of the witnesses agreed that blacks having a qualification in terms of section 10(1) (a), (b) or (c) of the act are more choosey than workers admitted on contract . . . In practice it was found that he would rather remain without work than fill a vacancy not to his liking, whether he was suited for it or not . This excessive choosiness often degenerated into work-shyness because of long periods of unemployment forced those concerned to find a living in other ways, for example by gambling, prostitution, smuggling, etc. On the other hand this phenomenon was not found among Section 10(1) (d) blacks, because their presence in an urban area was coupled with employment for a particular employer for a particular time, and for this reason employers preferred these blacks.[18]

The method recommended to curb this "work-shyness" was to increase the costs of living in the black urban areas. Africans who by "right" live there would then be forced to take jobs in order to be able to afford to live there:

58

There is some merit in the argument of certain witnesses that urban blacks should themselves bear a greater share of the total financial burden in respect of housing, services and transport. If this were done, the necessity for a regular monthly wage income would be heightened and persons could hardly afford to stay unemployed.[19]

This suggestion was adopted by the government in its subsequent White Paper:

The Department of Plural Relations and Development, the administration boards and community councils should initiate purposeful programmes of action in order to recover more and more of the cost of services from the black communities themselves.[20]

Thus, the urban elite too would be subject to control, albeit primarily economic rather than legal.

As we have seen, the Riekert Commission planned to tighten influx control by concentrating on controlling jobs and housing. As this control became more effective, the Commission felt it would be possible to remove some of the more obnoxious regulations imposed upon the black population.

Riekert recommended eliminating the new "Idle Bantu" clause which brings severe penalties against any person declared an "Idle Bantu": including loss of Section 10 rights and forced labour for up to two years. It found that the law was not being used, since the "nature of the Section 29 enquiry is sometimes confused with that of criminal proceeding by the courts, which require . . . a wealth of facts to be proved before a "conviction" is upheld . . ."[21]

It also recommended repealing the curfew regulations. Under these, the State President can declare the public sections of an area closed to Africans during the specified hours of the night (from 9 or 10 p.m. to 4 or 5 a.m., usually) unless the African has written permission from his employer or other authority. As of May 1977 night permits were required in 309 "prescribed" (white) areas: only 39 areas did not require permits. Riekert argued that "for emergency situations there is already adequate provision for the introduction of a curfew regulation that would apply to all population groups".[22]

It was recommended that any African found "illegally" in an urban area be simply deported to his bantustan, and not subjected to criminal proceedings which clog the courts and remove potential workers from the labour market. To effect this, it was proposed to expand the "aid centres" already functioning alongside present "pass law" courts.

Further, the Commission suggested that the 72-hour limit, beyond which an African is not allowed to stay in a "prescribed" area unless he is employed there or has Section 10(1) (a), (b) or (c) rights, be eliminated. The Commission felt it would become redundant; if "illegal" workers could find neither jobs nor housing they would have no reason to stay in the urban area.

Finally, Riekert did not recommend doing away with passes. Instead, it looked forward to the time when a pass would be something carried by the elite urban African only—migrants and bantustan citizens would carry travel documents from their "own governments". Thus the image of the pass would change, it was hoped, becoming a "prestige" document. Both passes and travel documents would of course still hold the vital employment and accommodation authorizations (although perhaps not a full record of employment, as the labour bureaux would have these at a centralized place). The Commission did not comment on whether a pass should have fingerprints, as they do now.

The Riekert Commission felt that these measures would eliminate nearly all the "discriminatory" legislation of apartheid, leaving effective control through housing and accommodation. However, one law had to be retained for Africans only, to enable the proposed control of housing and employment to provide an effective means of influx control for Africans (while not seriously affecting the rest of the population). The regulations of Section 10(1) of the Blacks (Urban Areas) Consolidation Act must stay. We have seen how again and again this plays a key role. Since only Africans are not allowed in the prescribed areas freely, only Africans would be excluded if they are unemployed, and only Africans would be by law unable to find accommodation in the urban areas.

The government however did not accept the Riekert Commission Report absolutely. The Government White Paper fully endorsed the recommended method of influx control—through housing and employment, tightening up the labour bureaux system and forcing registration by harsher penalties against the employers of "illegals". But it seemed rather reluctant to let go some of the other measures of control that the Riekert Commission believed to be super-fluous.

The White Paper stated the government would not eliminate pass laws penalties (i.e. fines and endorsing out) for illegal African residents in the pre-scribed areas:

> Penalties applicable to the worker also have a preventative effect in that they may deter the worker from entering the urban area unlawfully ...
> The government ... does not want to commit itself at this stage to repealing the 72-hour provision [*limiting Africans to 72 hours in a prescribed area if they are not covered by Section* 10][3], but would rather retain this third element of the influx control mechanism for the time being. If the stricter application of the other two elements ... proves effective ... the repeal of the 72-hour provision may be considered again.[23]

Early in 1980, the government announced it would experiment by relaxing the 72-hour law in the Bloemfontein and Pretoria areas. Later the government amended this saying that instead of dropping the 72-hour law in these areas, it would only conduct a "test survey" on the matter in these areas, "with the view to establishing the further practicability or otherwise" of dropping the law. As an opposition Member of Parliament commented:

> My impression ... is that for every step forward, there has been an equiva-lent step backwards. And this I think is a classical example.[24]

The curfew regulation, the government agreed, should be eliminated. On the other hand, the White Paper did not accept without qualification the repeal of Section 29 (the Idle Bantu Clause); it felt that more study was necessary before it could be sure the Act was redundant. The government was also unwilling to repeal the Black Resettlement Act of 1954, under which Africans have been removed from urban areas en masse. The Government felt this could only be dropped from the books when "it has served its purpose in respect of certain remaining cases".[25]

The government White Paper wholeheartedly accepted the idea of placing more of the burden of costs of services upon the urban African.

At the time of writing, the Riekert Commission's recommendations have not yet been fully integrated into the law. The legal situation is rather complex, some amendments being dealt with by ministerial proclamation and some having to go through Parliament. Some restrictions may be administrative procedures which can be changed without legal process at all, at the discretion of the bureaucracy.

The first and most important step taken by government towards implementing the Riekert Report was to pass a law penalizing the employer who fails to register his African employee by a R500 fine. This was supposed to go into effect from 13.7.79. However, the public outcry reached such large proportions that a "moratorium" was called until 31 October, during which time employees who had worked for one employer illegally for over one year, or for several employers for over three years, could be registered without facing penalties. (This concession was not applicable to the Western Cape—a "Coloured Labour Preferential Area".)[26]

Under the "temporary reprieve", WRAB registered over 500 people in one day, and over 10,000 in the first four weeks.[27] The fine was clearly already changing the structure of employment for Africans.

The *Financial Mail* summed up the non-urban African's situation as follows: to remain "legal" he must find work on a one-year contract, which must be re-registered each year; WRAB stated that domestic and heavy labourers usually meet no difficulties in registering contracts. Applicants must, however, also prove they have accommodation (a hostel bed or lodger's permit), which only the legally employed can get. The easiest solution to these bureaucratic requirements is that the employer reserve hostel beds.[28]

At the end of October, the "moratorium" ended. The non-urban African now had to follow the system of influx control laid down by the Riekert Commission, or go unemployed. The Black Sash, increasingly concerned with the plight of urban Africans, in November published the following in an Emergency Report:

> Never in the sixteen years since this office was opened have we experienced such anger expressed by black people or such a sense of impending catastrophe . . .
>
> Up to now the only saving factor for the people has been the total inefficiency of the system. All the vast ponderous and expensive structure of influx control and efflux enforcement has not been able to prevent people from moving to places where they could find work. They have been compelled

by the necessity of earning a living for themselves and for the survival of their children, and illegal jobs have been readily available . . .
Until this year people have been able to find illegal work and so have survived. Now, for the first time in all our experience we have no hope and no comfort to offer to the unregistered and the endorsed out. Always before we and they have known that they would be able to go on somehow even if it meant arrest and imprisonment from time to time. All hope has now been removed and when you take hope away all that is left is rage and anger, bitterness and hatred . . .[29]

The second aspect of the Riekert Report which has been instituted, although in a more piece-meal fashion, is the recommendation that urban Africans be made to "bear a greater share of the financial burden".

Rents have risen drastically. A few examples: Sakhile township near Standerton, still using a bucket system for sewerage and a community tap for water, had rents raised from R9.47 to R17.47 per month for a normal administration board house; families occupying houses they built themselves pay R11.30 instead of the previous R4.30 as "site rental".[30] ERAB announced across the board rises in rent, water and electricity. In one East Rand township, Daveyton, rents were to go up from R23.71 to R29.81 by 1 January 1980.[31] In Soweto's Dobsonville, the community council announced staggered rent rises: from R13.78 to R22.75 by 1 September 1979; to R30.15 by 1 November; to R37.55 by 1 January 1980.[32] Not surprisingly this announcement was met with outrage, and just before Prime Minister Botha's well-publicized flying visit to Soweto, Dr. Koornhof promised rents would not go up.[33] However a month afterwards, Dobsonville Community Council Chairman Steve Kgame was attacked by an "angry crowd" after attempting to "explain" the new rent increases to them.[34] WRAB also announced plans to introduce a new water tariff. For a four-room house on the West Rand the new rent plus rates could run as high as R70 per month; people fear they will pay out over R100 after the introduction of electricity. The new "luxury" houses (a normal four-room house plus internal bath and toilet) in Kagiso and Mohlakeng can be rented for R50 plus R16 water tariff (with an extra R80 connection fee for the water).[35]

These rates should be compared to the average income for an urban African household of five, of R158 per month in 1977. The average monthly wage in March 1978 (for an African engaged in industry) was R149.

Further, there have been attempts across the country to raise bus fares. Between 1977 and 1978 bus fares increased by 50% in Johannesburg.[36] In Cape Town bus companies applied for permission to increase the fares by 100%; the Supreme Court however ruled this out of order (although some rises would be acceptable).[37] PUTCO bus company in Pretoria is to raise its fares by 16%.[38] In Port Elizabeth, civic leaders warned the government that there would be renewed violence, following the 1976–1977 pattern, if fare rises of 20% to 40% were put into effect.[39]

It is clear that the recent "concessions" form only one aspect of a strategy that adds up to increasing repression of the African population as a whole. The small number of richer Africans may now buy themselves out of some of the discomforts of their situation as Africans, under apartheid. The bulk of the African population, the poor, the unemployed, the migrant labour, lose the loopholes in legislation that enabled many of them to survive in the past.

The Black Sash Emergency Report of November 1979 pointed out:

People are not going to go and sit to watch their sons and daughters die of hunger. They will remain in town, and, as they are hounded from their place of illegal accommodation (another of Dr. Riekert's recommendations) their rage will be fuelled to fuel again the rage of those who are legally in town and to whom so many promises have been made but not fulfilled.[40]

SECURITY

Repression

The new government policy means a stricter enforcement of apartheid. This in turn requires an even more repressive attitude towards internal dissent.

The government pours money into the military and security services to counter the threat of outright insurgency. At the same time, the government has also taken other steps to quell any internal demands from those who have not accepted the "new dispensation". The more "moderate" African leaders have been offered a role in "consulting" government bodies; others however, still face the repressive measures for which South Africa has long been known. In the year ending 30 June 1978, 21,217 people were tried for crimes against the state (public violence, unlawful and riotous assembly, sabotage, inciting or promoting unrest, arson and malicious damage to property); of these 14,390 were convicted.[1]

Detentions, bannings and political trials continue unabated. In its annual list of banned persons, in July 1979, the government named 154 people, 39 whites and 115 blacks.[2] Several of these have left the country, prohibited from pursuing their political activities because of the bans and in many cases having lost their employment as well.

Detentions need not be publicized under South African law. In May 1979 65 persons were known to be detained under Section Six of the Terrorism Act (providing for indefinite detention for interrogation); 13 of these 65 were held since 1978. 23 people were held under Section 12b of the 1976 Internal Security Act as potential witnesses in security trials; four people were listed as held under the General Law Amendment Act providing for 14-day detention.[3]

One series of detentions that deserves special mention: South Africa commemorated Steve Biko's death in detention a year later, in September 1978, by detaining nearly all of his adult relatives—his younger sister and her husband, his brother, and at least fourteen other relatives and friends.[4]

The government had previously cracked down on a Catholic Youth Group, the Young Christian Workers (YCW) with 30 detentions between May and June 1978, including the general secretary, the Transvaal regional secretary, and the entire Vereeniging and Kroonstad committees. Two members were later charged with sabotage, although eventually freed on appeal. The South African Catholic Bishops Conference reported to the Vatican that the government's action against the YCW constituted "a covert attack on the church in South Africa".[5]

Over the past two years, several new black organizations have been formed, to take the place of those banned in October 1977. These have suffered from the same official repression: members arrested, detained, banned. The Azanian Peoples Organization (AZAPO) was created on 1 May 1978; by 4 May two executive officers were detained, and by 1 June all of AZAPO's national officers as well as the officials of the Bloemfontein and Welkom branches were in detention. AZAPO had so many detentions and bannings within its membership that it could not hold its inaugural conference until seventeen months after its formation, in September 1979.[6]

The newest of South Africa's black organizations, the Congress of South African Students, (COSAS) for secondary school students, was founded in June 1979. In December the president and six executive members were detained. AZAPO's statement in response to these detentions reads:

> It is extraordinary to talk of (racial) conciliation while a total onslaught is waged against leaders of the Congress of South African Students.[7]

The one apparent improvement in government repression has been the drastic drop in the number of people who have died in detention. In 1977, 14 people died in detention; in 1978 following the Biko death and inquiry, one died. In 1979 none died. However, this only refers to people who died in political detention—161 people died "awaiting trial" in police custody in 1978, compared to 128 people in 1977.[8] Since often people are not recorded as "detained" unless the police are pressured (for instance if the person is well-known), it is commonly believed that police merely record dead prisoners as "awaiting trial" instead of "detained". The one person listed as killed in detention in 1978, Lungile Tabalaza, either fell or was thrown from the security police offices in Port Elizabeth into the crowded streets below, a situation the police could hardly disguise.[9] Further, people can simply disappear: the Botswana government in 1979 named four Botswana citizens who were detained in South Africa in October 1977, and have not been heard of since, although the South African police claim they were released the following day.[10]

The use of political trials as a means of repression has also continued, with increasing numbers of those on trial being accused of military action and intent, indicative of the numbers of trained guerillas who are now returning to South Africa and who are not accorded prisoner-of-war status if captured. Solomon Mahlangu, an ANC member who left South Africa in 1976, was hanged for murder in April 1979, after a white man had been killed in a fight with three ANC guerillas, despite evidence that Mahlangu had not actually fired a weapon.

James Mange, another ANC combatant is at the time of writing awaiting execution for guerilla actions. After the hanging of Mahlangu, the *Post* wrote:

Today we weep for Solomon Mahlangu . . . The man Jesus died a week after Solomon met his death in Pretoria. Perhaps today he is in paradise with that man Jesus.[11]

This suggests that the African people regard young militants like Mahlangu as heroes and martyrs rather than terrorists.

The South African government has also increased its battery of repressive legislation.

The ban on all outdoor public meetings (other than sports meetings and those with special permission) was extended once more in 1979 for a year; it has been in continuous existence since 1976.

Parliament has passed an amendment to the Police Act introducing a fine of up to R10,000 or five years in prison for publishing untruths about the police, with the burden of proof to lie with the press. The law also created a "press liaison officer" to check that stories give the "correct" perspective. The Inquests Act has been amended to bring inquests under the sub judice rule which means that the press are hindered in commenting on the cause of deaths in detention (such as that of Steve Biko) until the inquest finding is reached.[12]

Restrictions on press reporting have increased in other ways. Anyone publishing information on fuel supplied to South Africa is subject to 7 years' imprisonment. A legal twist added in 1977 which received practically no attention at the time: under a law dating from 1917 ("Section 83") a journalist must reveal his or her sources of information before a magistrate. From 1977, the penalties for refusing to do this are two years in jail for non-security matters and five years (maximum) for security matters . . . but if on release the journalist continues to refuse to reveal those same sources he or she may be resentenced to another two or five years respectively.[13]

The government has also created a new post of Advocate-General to examine allegations of corruption and malpractice against the government (following the Department of Information scandal). Statements before the Advocate-General have to be sworn, eliminating "even the best sources if those sources insist on anonymity"; and the government has implied that any matter taken up by the Advocate-General automatically becomes sub-judice and thus closed to the press. The opposition maintains:

. . . the creation of an advocate-general could easily be used to hamper the press in the exercise of its watchdog function. The proposal could, in fact, be the Prime Minister's promised legislation against "rumour-mongering" in another form.[14]

Censorship action against certain papers has continued, although it is notable that the *Post* newspaper has to a large extent stepped into the shoes of the banned *World*. The *Sunday Post* in particular is proving forthright and militant in its reporting. Other journals have suffered from official action.

65

In June 1978 the government banned the ecumenical weekly, the *Voice*. The banning was then lifted on condition that all issues be viewed by the Directorate of Publications within twelve hours of publication. The *Star* editorial reporting the banning of the *Voice* was headlined: "If it speaks, ban it", and concluded: "The government is methodically banning voiced of black dissent—black organization, much black writing, some theatre. None of these bans solves anything. They simply drive the dissent underground or into exile".[15]

The paper of the Inkatha movement, the *Nation*, was forced temporarily to suspend publication following five successive issues meeting the censor's axe in 1979, and the black writers' magazine, *Staffrider*, has had two issues banned. The *Post* commented:

> We are living under the spectre of mass bannings and eventually complete closures as did happen to some papers we have been close to. History may very well repeat itself and tomorrow we may wake up with the sad news that another paper has been completely shut down . . .
>
> Banning of newspapers is most unfair, especially with the minefield of laws and restrictions that editors have to tread through with almost undignified dread before their papers hit the streets.[16]

Most recently, church and state have come into confrontation. The South African Council of Churches (SACC), in its tenth national conference in July 1978, discussed such subjects as: "South Africa in crisis—our response as Children of God" and foreign investment. The Institute of Race Relations reported that "The SACC was subjected to continued attacks by the Afrikaans press and the South African government"[17], leading to fears that government measures against the SACC would follow. The president of the SACC, Bishop Tutu, has been questioned by security police and deprived of his passport; the vice-president, Mrs Sally Motlana (wife of Dr. Motlana of the Soweto Committee of Ten) was detained under Section Six of the Terrorism Act in October 1978. Early in 1980, government began to "warn" the SACC in unequivocal terms, and churchmen were among those arrested.[18]

CONCEALMENT

The last facet of the Botha government's "Save South Africa" formula consists of concealment and confusion—so that no-one is quite clear what, if anything, is being altered. "Facts and figures" are issued apparently invented out of thin air; "changes" are announced which never occur, or turn out to be only a change in name. Some of this, no doubt, reflects disagreements within the government: a change is announced and then rescinded or watered down until it becomes ineffectual when a proposal evokes a very negative response in the white population. But some can only be explained as outright lies.

Musical Names

A prime example of such "change" is in the name-changing employed by government bodies. The Department of Bantu Affairs and Development in early 1978 changed its name to the Department of Plural Affairs and Development, leading to many rude comments about "Bantus" evolving into "plurals". By March the Department asserted that "Bantu" remained the official term in all uses except the Ministry's title. The new Minister Dr. Koornhof invited new suggestions, and finally chose the "Department of Co-operation and Development". The substance of the department of course remains constant throughout.

In 1979, the term "Black" replaced "Bantu" and "Native" in all official usage in South Africa: retrospectively the Natives Land Act of 1913 becomes the Black Land Act of 1913, and the Bantu (Urban Areas) Consolidation Act becomes the Black (Urban Areas) Consolidation Act.

The Riekert Commission hoped to change the name of the Bantu Administration Boards, at present simply Administration Boards, to Regional Boards for Black Community Development, "in order to fit in with the designation and spirit of the proposed Black Community Development Act".[1]

The Bureau for State Security, popularly known throughout the world as BOSS, has been changed to the Department of National Security (DONS), and then to the Department of National Intelligence (DONI). ("BOSS" however remains the popular term.)

The Bantu Education Department changed to the Department of Education and Training, and it was announced that "Bantu Education" was to be eliminated. The new "blacks-only education" many people consider hardly a major change. Yet it has been presented as a move towards the beginning of "compulsory free education". The Department of Education and Training reported:

The first step towards compulsory education was announced by the Minister in 1976. Basically this means that the parent enters into an agreement to keep his child at school for at least four years".[2]

Far from being a move towards a better education, most Africans viewed that particular measure as an attempt to break the 1976 school boycott, by putting upon the parent the onus of forcing students back into class.

The Ministry of Labour changed—on the Wiehahn Commission's recommendation—to the Ministry of Manpower Utilization.

The Big Lie

Another aspect of the concealment and confusion is the South African government's use of the exaggeration technique—if you make a big enough claim people will believe it. Government spokesmen tend to make well-publicised announcements on facets of apartheid which later turn out to be hollow.

For example, the government in early 1979 announced the forthcoming end of the pass system. But the actual change proposed was that passes were to be replaced by "documents similar to those used by whites"; influx control would remain the same.[3] In other words, the shape of the pass would change, but blacks would still be fingerprinted, and they would still need permits for residence, for employment, for travel. (This is not the first time a Nationalist government has done this: the present pass is the result of the 1952 "Abolition of Passes Act"). The *Sunday Post* commented:

> Here comes the all-new-just-as-dompas. Some say it's the greatest break-through in race relations since the new number plate system was introduced (*substituting numbers for letters on car licence plates*). On the other hand, those with a sense of humour, like Dr. Piet, probably see it as a means of tightening-up influx control.[4]

Six months later, in July 1979, Dr. Piet Koornhof told an American audience:

> I have declared war on the dompas. The thing must be ousted completely out of my country and I have told my officials to work on it . . . I am working on a month time-span not a year time-span.[5]

That same month pass raids were conducted on a weekly basis throughout the Reef, Free State and Cape.[6] Today, the pass laws remain unchanged.

Misrepresentation is pervasive. The Wiehahn Report was hailed as extending trade union "rights" to all Africans, whereas the legislation extends trade union membership as a possible privilege, dependent upon the goodwill of the registrar towards the African union concerned. The Riekert Report was hailed as a step forward in race relations in general and in the legal status of the African in particular; as we saw above, it has been disastrous for both. On the level of practice, we find that even those concessions announced as "accepted" by the government White Paper on the Riekert Commission have not in fact been instituted. The government White Paper accepted that wives who do not qualify under Section 10(1) (a) or (b) could join husbands who did so qualify if housing was available. But, as was pointed out:

> Neither Board (WRAB or ERAB) will accept a man on the waiting list to rent a house unless his wife has a permit to be in that area and she cannot get a permit unless he has a house.[7]

Or again:

> Dr. Koornhof has said that Dr. Riekert's recommendation that Section 10—qualified urban people can move from one town to another provided they have a job and accommodation is already in operation. The West Rand Board is endorsing them out (*i.e. treating such people as illegal migrants*).[8]

In this context, Dr. Piet Koornhof, now Minister of Co-operation and Development, deserves special mention. As Minister of Sport he was renowned for conflicting statements. As Minister of Co-operation and Development he has found more scope for this talent. Mr. Hassan Howa, president of the South African Council of Sport, was quoted as saying blacks should "never ever" trust Dr. Koornhof as "He was the kind of man who says what his audience expect of him."[9] A very clear picture of his methods came out with the publication of details of his talks with Crossroads squatter camp leaders over the "new dispensation" he had promised them:

> Transcripts of the meetings reveal Koornhof's intriguing style of diplomacy. Though he repeatedly stressed the need for trust and co-operation, dis-

cussion or questions were barely tolerated. Frequent references to his guidance from God impressed the highly religious Crossroads representatives, so too did an interesting game of charades in which he was actually reprimanded in front of them by another Minister for his softness and insistence upon compromise.

But his paternalism did not pass entirely unnoticed. "What Koornhof does is break you down", one delegate said later. "He hammers you one moment and then is nice to you. Eventually you are so relieved with the man being nice to you that you don't have to fight with him, and you somehow try to see his point of view. The whole thing is brilliant.[10]

Glenmore, the "model township"

In terms of simple human misery, the worst discrepancy between words and reality hangs over the "temporary township" (resettlement camp) of Glenmore, in the Eastern Cape.

The government has for some time planned to remove people from Grahamstown's black townships to the Ciskei. In 1977 the Department of Bantu Administration and Development said firmly that:

> In view of the fact that Grahamstown is less than 50km away from the Ciskei, policy dictates that Bantu families residing there should eventually move to the homelands concerned.[11]

The Grahamstown townships consist of some 200,000 people. Some of these people, such as the 300 black property owners of Fingo Village, have legal freehold title to the land. It was originally planned to move the 200,000 to Committee's Drift in the Ciskei. Dr. Koornhof announced it would be "the finest black town in South Africa".[12] The Ciskei protested against this move vehemently; the government then shelved its Committee's Drift plans "due to lack of funds". In 1976 Glenmore was chosen as an alternative site, across the valley from Committee's Drift. Glenmore is not yet part of the Ciskei, but is scheduled to become so eventually. The Ciskei again protested, but was silenced by promises to provide proper irrigation and infrastructure for the township. In September 1978 work began; by mid-1979 five hundred "temporary" houses had been constructed, with wooden walls, asbestos roofs, and mud floors. Plans were being promulgated for a total of 5,000 houses, including an "elite suburb" where people could buy plots on 99-year leases, to build houses of their choice.[13] The government promised to spend R29 million on the township, employing the first-come residents to build the houses for the later arrivals.[14] A new economic sub-centre would be born, a "model township".

In April 1979 the first 170 families were moved to Glenmore from a farm in Klipfontein where they had been squatting with the owner's approval. By June there were 3,000 people living in Glenmore.

The press was barred from Glenmore, but stories were soon picked up. People complained they were hungry—rations were distributed for the first few days only—and had fallen ill after drinking from the Glenmore water supply.[15]

69

The township used buckets for sewerage, with 25 people to a bucket "at a conservative estimate".[16] By 15 May, of the 489 families in the township, only 30 men had jobs, and these were rotated among the residents to distribute the wealth more evenly.[17] By June, there were reported to be 40 jobs among 3,000 people. A survey of 25 households in Glenmore showed that incomes had dropped from an average of R60 per family before moving to Glenmore to R27 per family per month after moving; several families in Glenmore had no cash at all. The difference was the result of loss of part-time work by wives, loss of jobs by husbands because of the distance to Grahamstown, greater expenses and so on.[18] Instead of the R29 million claimed, only R6 million had been allotted for the township, of which only a fraction was actually spent.[19]

On 12 April, Mr. Louis Koch, Chief Director of the Eastern Cape Administration Board stated:

> We believe that in moving the squatters here (to Glenmore) we have succeeded in bringing dignity to the lives of people who have been living in very unfavourable conditions".[20]

By 7 June, nine children had died from causes listed as gastro-enteritis, kidney infection, kwashiorkor and bronchial pneumonia (all of which reflect in part malnutrition).

In August, in the face of growing protest, Dr. Koornhof halted removals to Glenmore pending investigation by his department.[21] Certainly there was remarkably little correlation between the official government pronouncements and the realities of Glenmore.

It is, of course, probable that at least some of the differences between the government's words and deeds are not intentional. The administrative bureaucracy continues in its paths without necessarily referring to political statements made over its head. But there does seem to be an inordinate amount of outright falsehoods in government pronouncements.

Further, part of the technique is to announce proposed changes amid worldwide publicity; retractions or qualifications never receive the same coverage. In this way the "liberal" press in South Africa and the Western media help to propagate the fiction that apartheid is fading. The fact is that repression is intensifying.

The "New Apartheid"

The changes introduced by the Botha government have been proclaimed as a "new dispensation" for blacks. We have seen in a detailed examination of these concessions that nearly all involve possibly exempting a small number of Africans from the apartheid laws, rather than actually eliminating those laws; the "concessions" create privileges for a few rather than rights for all. But in addition, the new government's changes constitute an interlocking whole, which in total form a new and more effective stranglehold upon the African population.

Those Africans with urban residence qualifications (Section 10(1) (a) and (b)) gain the apparent benefits from the concessions. They select the community councils; but the councils have power only at the discretion of the Minister, and can only implement existing apartheid policies. These urban Africans can own houses in urban areas on 99-year leasehold; but these are expensive and above all dependent upon the owner retaining his Section 10 qualifications. Also, the home-ownership scheme has virtually blocked the availability of less expensive rented housing. Costs of living in black urban areas have risen drastically, but these rises have in no way been matched by increasing wages. Trade union privileges (definitely not rights) are to be available for Africans, but the government sees the operation of the trade union laws as an additional means of controlling African unions; they also appear to expect these unions to restrict themselves to non-migrants in their own interests. There are to be more permits granted giving exemption from the segregation laws of apartheid, but these mainly affect the small elite and, of course, have no effect at all upon the basic separation of facilities that constitutes apartheid. Black businessmen may operate more freely than previously, but still only in black areas.

At the same time as the government has handed the urban African these "concessions", it has undermined the Section 10 "rights" upon which such Africans rely. Section 10(1) (a), (b) and (c) rights are now not applicable to people from an "independent" bantustan if their parents came from that bantustan. Since eventually all the bantustans will be forced to take "independence", according to government statements, there will eventually be almost no black South African citizens at all—and Section 10 "rights" may be irrelevant. At the moment, however, it remains unclear what the government's real intention is for the urban African as far as citizenship is concerned. On a more immediate timescale, anyone unemployed for more than four months (not consecutively) out of the year may lose his Section 10 qualification, and may be removed to a rural area or put in a farm colony for up to two years.

The rural Africans (which eventually may include everyone) have been granted no privileges at all. Rather, they are offered a straight-jacket system of contract labour to the white areas for one year at a time, without the possibility of bringing their families because accommodation is provided for the labourer only; without the possibility of searching for employment on their own, but forced to take labour bureaux offers; without any of the social services of benefits generated by the "white" South African economy in which they labour. As *Post* commented in April 1979:

> We are not awaiting that "fate too ghastly to contemplate". We are already living it.[22]

Conclusion

The crucial question, of course, is will this plan succeed? It has definite advantages for the apartheid state if it can be implemented. However, it has met with opposition from several directions and the government's ability to carry through the formula is questionable.

Advantages of these changes for the white regime

The advantages of these changes for the white regime can be easily seen. First, they provide excellent propaganda for South Africa's campaign abroad for support, giving fuel to those who would block sanctions on South Africa, and to those transnational companies who maintain that investment in South Africa can work "against apartheid" from within it.

The most significant sign of this came in December 1979 when the Prime Minister of Britain, Mrs. Margaret Thatcher, proclaimed that:

> There is now a real prospect that the conflicts on South Africa's borders, in Rhodesia and Namibia, will shortly be ended. This combined with welcome initiatives on South Africa's domestic policies, offer a chance to defuse a regional crisis which was potentially of the utmost gravity, and to make progress towards an ending of the isolation of South Africa in World Affairs.[1]

Internally, the creation of a black "middle class" is designed to split African solidarity, setting the more secure township elite against the unskilled and unemployed majority. Urging employers to provide better training facilities, Dr. Koornhof in August 1979 said "such artisans would be politically and socially more disciplined, more conservative and less radical in their outlook".[2] By offering such people a small stake in prosperity, the state hopes to buy in their support (or at least acquiescence) for the system. Because of the high level of unemployment, and increasing poverty in the bantustans, some observers believe that the creation of the elite is intended to lead to conflict between the deprived and the relatively "privileged" Africans.

The "new deal" policy also accords with the interests of big business, which wants to be allowed to train and promote some employees whatever their colour into managerial and white-collar jobs, and to move them from area to area without the complications of the present pass-laws. At the same time, the big mining and manufacturing concerns need a cheap and docile manual labour supply which can be turned on and off as necessary, and which will not be a charge on public funds in times of unemployment, sickness or old age—as is being created in the bantustans. The new policy further strengthens the position of transnational corporations which wish to use South Africa as a basis for economic penetration of independent Africa to the north.

In November 1979 the Prime Minister, Mr. P. W. Botha, appealed publicly to big business for support from the private sector for the government's policies. Mr. Harry Oppenheimer, head of the Anglo-American Corporation, welcomed the proposed "new deal".[3]

The "right-wing backlash"

Perhaps the most immediate of the forces opposing the South African government's new plans are those whites who see the proposed changes as a threat to their privileges—the so-called "right-wing backlash". The white population of South Africa has supported white superiority for so long that even the slightest dent in their bulwark of legal protection against black equality appears dangerous. The extent of this "backlash" is not very clear, but one indication of white sentiment came in a by-election in November 1979 when the Nationalists lost their first parliamentary seat in a by-election since they came to power in 1948. (Admittedly this equally reflects disillusionment with the Nationalist Party over the Information Department scandal, as well as "confusion" over the new "liberal race policies", but commentators have primarily attributed the by-election defeat to the white backlash.)

White trade unions have been the most prominent wing of this backlash. In March 1979, white miners went on a series of wildcat strikes in what the English papers dubbed a "last ditch" attempt to retain job discrimination by law. The strikes collapsed within a week, without undue pressure from law enforcement agencies. Rather, the government agreed to a compromise by which the remaining job discrimination laws would be "phased out" in consultation with the unions involved.[4]

As of November 1979 five job reservation determinations remained. The white unions are no longer quite so unyielding. The (white) Underground Officials Association—in defiance of the Mine Workers Union—has agreed to accept the scrapping of Determination 27, which barred Africans from positions as mine surveyors, samplers and ventilation officials. They insisted, however, on the condition that they had the right to organize Africans entering these jobs, "so that we can ensure that they are not exploited and that our members are not undercut". The MWU has said they will fight the elimination of Determination 27 in the courts, as an "unfair labour practice".[5]

African Resistance

But a more significant obstacle to the government's plan to preserve apartheid is the reaction of the African population.

The designated "black middle class" has shown remarkable reluctance to accept the concessions offered. As we saw, Dr. Koornhof's offers to talk to black leaders were resoundingly rejected by all except community council members and bantustan leaders. African spokesmen have also rejected the "Black Education" that was to replace "Bantu Education". They have shown strikingly little interest in the home ownership scheme. This reaction is hardly surprising:

> How real, in any case, are the benefits to be enjoyed by an urban black with the proper papers ? He cannot vote a man into the Cape Town parliament. If he is a businessman he cannot trade freely in the white areas, or own a factory there. He has no freehold rights to his property. His children, if they have had homeland citizenship conferred upon them, and were born after their designated "black state" became independent, cannot inherit his lease or his rights to residence. What white father would stand it ?[6]

Another indication of rejection came at the show-piece Anglo-American mine at Elandsfontein. This mine represented private enterprise's attempts to give a lead to government: it incorporated "all the best thinking by mine planners, personnel, experts and architects in the 'single men's village' ", in an effort to demonstrate the advantages of a more stable, better-off black workforce.[7] Anglo-American had stated that this would be a "model" for future mine development, in line with their policy of introducing capital-intensive techniques which, the company claims, require greater stability and more training of labour.

On 8 April 1979, the day before the official opening of the Elandsfontein mine (the mine itself was already functioning) the black workforce erupted in violence and arson. Five hundred miners had to be quelled by mine security men and police reinforcements, dogs and a helicopter, in a two-and-a-half-hour battle. The next morning only 100 out of the 4,400 men went to work, and 800 were sent home permanently. It was reported (although newsmen were barred from talking to miners themselves) that the causes were low pay and food disputes. Again the "reforms" were simply not sufficient.[8]

But the "new deal" is not composed only of concessions. The African population has, predictably, reacted even more negatively to the repressive measures accompanying these concessions: the reinforcement of Grand Apartheid, and the increase in the financial burdens of the urban African.

Rent and rates increases announced following the Riekert Report recommendations have evoked loud protests. The Soweto rent increases of over 300%, spread over 4 months, were first revoked by Dr. Koornhof, then reimposed by the community councils a month later.[9] Mr. David Thebahali, head of the Soweto Community Council, confessed that the community councils had no choice but to raise the rents, since the government had removed the housing subsidy.[10] The Soweto Committee of Ten then held a two-day conference, attended by some 1,000 people, to create the Soweto Civic Association. The SCA would replace the Committee of Ten by a mass-membership organization, with 33 branches throughout Soweto. The SCA announced it would fight the rent rises. In October, it decided to apply for a court injunction to halt the increases.[11] At the time of writing, the new rents have not yet been imposed; Soweto residents are adamant that they will resist them.

74

The tactic of the bus boycott, used effectively by the ANC in the 1950's, has been revived in response to increases in bus fares. In Ladysmith, Natal, the bus company attempted to impose higher fares: on 10 September the African population started a boycott. It rapidly spread to Hammarsdale, Port Shepstone, Newcastle, Dundee and Pietermaritzburg. 15,000 workers walked up to 50 km per day to and from work,[12] After two weeks of boycott and the loss of R140,000 the bus company agreed to return fares to their previous price and to transfer a disliked manager. The bus boycott however continued:

> The people don't want to know Ezakheni Transport. They are tired of them. Their prices are too high and their service is too poor. They want to get rid of Ezakheni Transport.[13]

In Port Shepstone and Margate, the Trans-Umzimkulu Bus Company announced 50% fare increases; on 18 September 950 workers staged a sitdown strike at a Margate factory for wage increases to cover this rise. The management called the police; violence ensued and the workers were finally cleared by tear gas.[14] Africans then boycotted Port Shepstone and Margate buses; by 1 October the buses were only 5% full.[15] By the fourth week the Port Shepstone Chamber of Commerce president reported local businesses were losing R100,000 a week due to the boycott,[16] and by the fifth week he telegrammed the national government that it had to take "urgent action".[17] After two months the bus boycotts were called off—at least temporarily—when Dr. Koornhof promised to instigate "negotiations" with the bus companies.

Perhaps the most interesting case study to date of the response to the "new apartheid" came with the Port Elizabeth strikes of late 1979. Black urban residents working in Port Elizabeth factories, especially in skilled and white collar jobs, should in theory be among those most likely to benefit from the "new deal". In fact, workers found the concessions offered to them too small, and implemented too slowly. At the same time, they faced the operation of another facet of the "new apartheid"—control over residence. The government planned to remove the long-established township of Walmer, with a population of 4,000 to 6,000, where many of the workers lived, and resettle them elsewhere:

> Compounding anger at the removal is the fact that Walmer is close enough to town for many people to be able to be within walking distance of their jobs, while Zwide Extension Four—the area to which the removal is due to take place—is farther out.
> In addition, Port Elizabeth's black townships already have a waiting-list running to more than 10,000.[18]

Unfulfilled promises of an end to apartheid, combined with further oppression under the apartheid laws, created a highly explosive situation in Port Elizabeth. On 30 October 1979, African residents of Port Elizabeth held the inaugural meeting of the Port Elizabeth Black Civic Organization, PEBCO (following the Soweto Civic Association formed the month before). PEBCO called for equal rights for all people in Port Elizabeth, and opposition to discriminatory legislation. It drew crowds of 10,000 to its meetings, and formed links with the

Soweto Committee of Ten and the Azanian People's Organization (AZAPO). PEBCO's chairman, Mr. Thozamile Botha, was a trainee draughtsman at the Port Elizabeth Ford plant, and thus potentially a member of the "new black middle class".

In early November, Ford told Mr. Botha to choose between his Ford job and his position as head of PEBCO. He resigned from Ford; and the 738 other members of the African workforce downed tools in protest. This put the company in a very difficult position for, being under pressure from abroad to end discrimination in its South African plants, it had gone much farther than other employers in this direction, integrating canteens and recognising the Black Union of Auto Workers, affiliated to the Federation of South African Trade Unions (FOSATU), the newest and most militant legal black union organization. So, in reaction to the strike, Ford unconditionally reinstated Mr. Botha, saying he had resigned "as a result of a misunderstanding".[19] The African workers then returned to work.

However, this did not end Ford's problems. The white workers of the South African Yster-en-Staal (Iron and Steel) Union complained that Ford conceded too much to African workers, and objected to integrated facilities. Black workers then protested about forced overtime (to correct "imbalances" caused by the previous stoppage) and white workers' attitudes. They demanded that Ford actually implement its official policy of equal pay for equal work. On 21 November African workers again downed tools. Ford called in squads of riot police, then told the assembled strikers to work or get out. The workers

. . . stood up en masse and surged through the gates chanting: "We're sacked" and raising their hands in the black power salute.[20]

The strikers formed a PEBCO-affiliated committee to negotiate with management.[21]

On 19 November 1979, the African workforce at the General Tire plant also in Port Elizabeth (owned by General Motors, USA) went on strike. They demanded union recognition, the reinstatement of two laid-off workers, and an end to discriminatory pay and employment practices and segregated facilities. On 22 November the entire black workforce of General Tire was sacked.[22]

African workers at the Adams Paper Mill in Port Elizabeth also struck on 22 November, demanding a higher minimum wage; four days later 250 of the 450 were sacked. By 7 December, all but 50 had been re-employed.[23]

Sacked workers from Ford and General Tire held a mass meeting, chaired by Mr. Thozamile Botha, to organize strike strategy. They determined not to return to work until all the workers were reinstated.[24] Following this, security police detained 29 workers (eight were released the next day). Twenty-four of these were later charged under the Riotous Asemblies Act.

On 12 December General Tire agreed to re-hire strikers. Ford however closed down for its annual Christmas break with some 500 workers still out. Ford workers appealed to workers in the parent plant in Detroit and to American civil rights leaders for support. When the factory reopened on 10 January, management conceded and reinstated all striking workers. The industrial unrest appeared settled.

The following day, Mr. Botha and three other PEBCO leaders were detained, while preparing for a meeting against the Walmer removals. A *Post* reporter was also detained after filing a report on these detentions. Riot police used teargas to disperse crowds protesting at the detentions; journalists were ordered out of the township and photographs of police actions were confiscated.[25]

At the time of writing, the issue of the removals (scheduled for June 1980) appears to have replaced that of working conditions as the focus of conflict. After the detention of PEBCO officials, a meeting of 3,000 members voted to begin a "stay-at-home" (general strike) in Port Elizabeth townships to protest at the removals and detentions:

> A mood of defiance has been growing in the township in the last few weeks, partly encouraged, no doubt, by the increasing militancy in Port Elizabeth's motor industry. Walmer residents now say that they will refuse to move.[26]

Elsewhere, strikes have spread during the first part of 1980.

The Port Elizabeth case shows African reaction to the "new apartheid" as a system, as an interrelated structure of concession and repression. This response has been one of rejection. The concessions are too minor. The repression that accompanies them—the rapidly rising cost of living in urban areas, combined with forced removals, and residential control, combined with enforced "independence" for the Bantustans and loss of citizenship—has led to increasingly militant resistance. Far from creating a black "buffer" against the revolution, the "new deal" so far has fed fuel to the forces opposed to the apartheid system.

The gold price

At this point, however, one must enter a caveat. With the gold fever of late 1979 and early 1980, the South African government suddenly found itself with unexpected wealth. "Every time gold clocks up another dollar in London, Pretoria's coffers swell by 13 million dollars in extra tax receipts from the mines, while Anglo-American, the largest of South Africa's seven mining houses, finds itself with another eight million dollars on its hands."[27] In early July 1979 the gold price was at $280 an ounce; it topped $1,000 an ounce in early 1980 before falling back to $700. Numerous observers have called upon the South African government to use this unexpected income to implement homeland consolidation to establish black housing schemes, to improve the townships, to provide free black education—in other words, to actually bring about the changes the government has announced over the last several years. But this would require time (as well as inclination) and time is in increasingly short supply. The alternative, to spend the extra money on tax relief for whites, fuel and armaments, to further entrench the present situation, may well appear more attractive to the South African government (as indeed the 1980 budget showed).

The Resistance Movement

The largest and most dangerous threat to such plans to save South Africa comes of course from the growing resistance movements, the ANC and PAC. Any chance the new formula has must be measured in terms of a race against time.

On 4 August 1978, African National Congress guerillas first skirmished with South African troops near Zeerust on the Botswana border. The ANC claimed 10 South African troops were killed; South Africa captured one guerilla, and did not admit to any losses. (The South African press is well-censored on all "terrorism" stories.) The defence forces used helicopters to search the area, which is hilly and covered with scrub; the ANC also reported that defoliants were sprayed to remove cover.[28]

Since then, there have been more clashes reported when small groups of well armed guerillas have been intercepted by South African army patrols. All of South Africa's borders are now permanently patrolled by the armed forces, sometimes with dogs. The number of clashes remains uncertain, since South Africa has not always announced them as they occur—they have admitted to four or five. They also have seized several weapons caches, presumably stored for future use. The South African press reported in March 1979, that Botswana police had arrested four black South Africans for possessions of arms: displayed in court were AK-47 rifles, three sub-machine guns, 47 blocks of explosives and a rocket launcher.[29] The independence of Zimbabwe completes the circle of independent states surrounding South Africa from which guerilla attacks could be launched.

Sabotage has become relatively common. In July 1979 the Defence Force acknowledged over 30 acts of sabotage committed over 12 months. This figure is probably rather low, for instance, in April 1979 an oil-carrying train blew up; the papers labelled it a "mystery explosion". A WRAB liquor store blown up in December 1978 was ascribed to burglary and arson rather than sabotage, despite eye-witness reports of an explosion.[30]

The South African Defence Force has estimated that the ANC has 4,000 people undergoing military training, mostly in Angola, and that many more leave South Africa each year.[31] The Pan Africanist Congress has also guerilla training camps, in Libya, China and Tanzania.

In May 1979, following the execution by South Africa of guerilla Solomon Mahlangu, an ANC force attacked a small Soweto police station in Moroka and demolished it, killing a policeman and escaping unscathed. In November 1979, a group of guerillas attacked the main Soweto police station in Orlando, killing three policemen while sixty off-duty police in a nearby barracks "hid under their beds rather than risk the dash to the main office where their guns were stored".[32]

As the *Guardian* pointed out:

> Ironically, the raid came only hours after the Minister for Black Affairs, Dr. Piet Koornhof, announced a new deal for black businessmen as part of a

master-plan to give blacks a better share in South Africa's wealth.[33] .
And as the defence White Paper tabled in Parliament in April 1979 remarked: "The military threat against South Africa is intensifying at an alarming rate".[34]

Conclusion

South Africa's "new dispensation" for Africans, then, provides no more than a face-lift: it attempts to give the Government a "new look" without altering the underlying structure of apartheid. Indeed, in many ways apartheid has grown stronger. Dr. Riekert called his new improved influx control "simplified and streamlined"; the Minister of Co-operation and Development reiterated in July 1979 that the African "would not obtain political rights in white South Africa". Dr. Motlana replied:

> One is hesitant to say he is grateful that Dr. Koornhof has now cleared the air with his statement . . . We are now quite obviously back to square one— doctrinaire, granite hard Verwoerd apartheid.[35]

The clearest affirmation of traditional apartheid values came from Prime Minister P. W. Botha in November 1979:

> "I say one man, one vote in this country is out. I now want to say something further: Don't try to do something unconstitutional or you will be sorry for yourself".[36]

In conclusion, it can be said that the Botha government has offered the African population some exemptions from the apartheid laws: it has not offered to change the laws. The more clearly this policy emerges, the more clearly emerges the African response. No solution can be accepted that does not give "one man one vote"; or that does not enable the people to control their own destiny. A few extra privileges for a small segment of the population will not save South Africa's apartheid system. Nor, in the end, will the increasingly severe repression that accompanies the concessions.

POSTSCRIPT September 1980

To what extent and in what ways the events of recent months have involved any significant change in the balance of forces cannot yet be assessed. But it is clear that the new developments have not altered the conditions described or the trends outlined in these pages. If anything, the events of 1980 underscore the analysis of the situation presented here.

This year has seen a nationwide upsurge of organised resistance comparable in extent to that of 1976, if not surpassing it. The state has responded with all the repressive means in its power, together with further moves to devise new ways of adapting apartheid to preserve minority rule. As before, these moves are presented as evidence of enlightenment and reform. Behind them, however, lies a sustained determination to suppress and defeat all forms of resistance.

The unity of different struggles, at work and in the townships, which characterised the strikes and campaigns against rent increases and forced removals at the end of 1979 (*see* pp. 75-77) showed itself still more visibly in the months that followed. The protests, boycotts, strikes and evident support for increased guerilla activity such as the simultaneous sabotage in June of the showpiece Sasol oil plants, together amounted to an open expression, on an unprecedented scale, of the complete rejection of the apartheid system. As in the earlier events, those who were intended to benefit from the claimed reforms were active in the struggles.

Along with the suppression of opposition, the regime's response was combined with attempts to divide the oppressed majority by means of a revision of the constitutional proposals outlined on pp. 33-35, and another version of the bantustan policy as part of the "constellation of states" idea. These proposals, along with some for restructuring regional and local government, are far-reaching but, at the time of writing, they remained confused and confusing and in several respects are explicitly presented as merely interim. It is far from clear how they will be implemented. The confusion is indicative of the problems which beset the apartheid regime as it tries to formulate policies which will bring about the "stability" it desires.

The traditional Cabinet committee system has been replaced by five permanent Cabinet Committees containing a considerable number of military representatives.[1] This, and the appointment of General Malan, Chief of the SADF, as Minister of Defence, have made the involvement of the military in politics more prominent, as has the widespread use of the term "total strategy". This term covers strategies and policies which are by and large those analysed in this book, coloured by an urgency resulting from the ever-increasing resistance inside South Africa and the changed situation in Southern Africa following the independence of Zimbabwe. The presence of the military in the government caps its involvement in every sphere in a process initiated in the early 1970's. The process is described in the IDAF Fact Paper *Apartheid War Machine*, published in April 1980, and illustrated by the joint military-police "crime-sweeps" described on p. 45.[2]

As far as the situation of the black majority is concerned, the promised reforms and the "death of apartheid" have not materialised. Conditions have rather worsened.

The widespread school boycott which began in April 1980 demonstrated that in the field of education few, if any, changes had been implemented, as is suggested on pp. 24-5. In many instances conditions have deteriorated, particularly in African and Coloured schools.

In April the Prime Minister confirmed in Parliament that the changes in the "influx control" system recommended by the Riekert Report were a "change in mechanism, not a change in policy".[3] The only really major proposal to have been implemented is still the R500 fine on employers taking on unregistered labour.[4] Further reports from Black Sash Advice Offices indicate that the pass laws are

80

being more strictly applied and that workseekers from rural areas are finding it more difficult to get jobs in urban areas.[5] The consequences of such restrictions and of other forms of "relocation" to the bantustans, with very high levels of black unemployment and the absence of employment opportunities in the bantustans, continue to be brought to light, both by researchers and by events like the recent drought in KwaZulu and elsewhere. The drought exacerbated and drew attention to a situation which was already critical in terms of poverty, starvation, infant mortality and morbidity, and which is a direct result of government policies.[6]

In the labour field there was a major wave of action involving many thousands of workers. In its response the state showed its determination to try to force workers into acceptance of its "conciliation machinery" and its readiness to use the existence of that machinery as a justification for strike-breaking.

As in the strikes in Port Elizabeth in December 1979, described on pp. 75-77, some notable victories were achieved by workers organising outside the government-approved framework,[7] and support in the townships again played an important part. But state intervention, already substantial, assumed increasing proportions, with the detention of union organizers, mass arrests of strikers for "illegally striking" and "riotous assembly", the deportation of striking contract workers to the bantustans, and the banning of leaflets produced to mobilise support for the strikers in the townships.[8] Police action was used to break the strike by 10,000 Johannesburg municipal workers after the Minister of Manpower Utilisation had declared that the strike had "by-passed the conciliation machinery".[9] 1,200 contract workers were put on buses at their hostels and despatched to the bantustans, and the president of their union arrested and charged, together with two other officers of the union, with "sabotage".[10]

Notably, in the wake of the setting up of a shop-steward system by three firms in the Eastern Cape motor industry in September, the Minister of Manpower Utilization said, in what was interpreted as a hint of change, that management should deal with whatever leadership group had credibility among the workers. But he insisted that black unions would have to be brought under "statutory control" to avoid them "becoming the prey of our enemies".[11]

The actions against trade unionists and workers were part of the suppression of the struggle on many fronts, in workplaces, educational institutions, in the townships. By the end of June 393 people had been detained under the security laws, according to the South African Institute of Race Relations. A number of leading figures in the black community had been banned (including Thozamile Botha and other PEBCO officers). All meetings "of a political nature" of more than ten people were prohibited for two and a half months. Arrests of protesting pupils and students and others took place by the hundred, while police attacks on meetings, with baton charges and teargas, were frequent. Police shootings were estimated by the press to have left over 40 people dead in Cape Town, Bloemfontein, Durban and the Eastern Cape. The full scale of the police actions

81

could not be known as still further restrictions were placed on access by the press to areas of police actions.[12]

As the repression intensified and the resistance spread, the Schlebusch Commission on the constitution issued an interim report in May containing a number of proposals almost immediately implemented by the government.[13] One result was the power to appoint 12 additional MPs to Parliament without the need for election, a device used in September to bring General Malan into the Cabinet and which contributed to the process by which the Prime Minister has restructured government and administration in a way that brings it more firmly under his control.[14]

There was also a scheme to pave the way for yet another "new political dispensation". Its centre-piece is a President's Council consisting of 60 White, Coloured, Indian and Chinese members appointed by the President. It is a purely consultative body and its creation was presented as an interim measure whose principal function appears to be to produce ideas for further constitutional developments.[15] In an unsuccessful attempt to avoid the rejection of the 1979 Constitution Bill, based on its exclusion of Africans (see p. 33) the Government proposed setting up a separate Black Advisory Council with which the President's Council could liaise. Faced with calls to include Africans on the President's Council, the Prime Minister explained that it was out of the question, "an insurmountable obstacle".[16]. As he had confirmed earlier in the year, his policies were turning out to be a reformulation of and not a move away from "separate development".[17] He insisted that while the Government was prepared to create consultative bodies for Coloured, African and Indian leaders, it was not prepared to do so on the condition that it accepted majority rule in South Africa. "If confrontation must come over that," he said "then it must come".[18]

With the failure of the proposal for a Black Advisory council to win any support, the Prime Minister dropped it and instead launched a new round of talks with bantustan leaders to promote the "constellation of states" version of bantustan policy.[19] While the propaganda for this emphasises the economic interdependence of all of South Africa and the impossibility of any part being a viably independent economic unit,[20] political "independence" remains a keystone of the policy. Senior Government officials confirmed that "non-independent" bantustans would be excluded from decision-making in the "multilateral development bank" which is to be the centre-piece of the scheme.[21]

A similar adherence to the basic principles of apartheid was evident in the launching of talks in September on a proposed mixed metropolitan government system to replace the present system of provincial and local government. "Reliable sources" made clear that the Government was prepared to negotiate details of the system with Coloured and Indian leaders; that Africans would be excluded as the Government was planning to create autonomous municipalities in the black urban areas; and that the metropolitan board scheme would stick to the group areas and separate development policies, but at the same time provide another forum where Whites, Indians and Coloureds would have some share in decision-making.[22]

Whatever else happened in the first part of 1980, apartheid was shown to be neither dead nor in the course of being destroyed by the regime. An increasing number of observers came to realise this. A *Times* journalist wrote in July: "For all Mr. Botha's talk of the need for change, what he essentially wants to do is to adapt apartheid to present-day conditions and certainly not to dismantle it",[23] while a review in August in the *Sunday Express* concluded: "The pattern which is emerging is a reformulation of the basic principles of apartheid while forging ahead with peripheral change and economic reform".[24]

More bitterly, the Editor of the *Post* wrote:

The Prime Minister's alleged bold initiatives have remained largely undefined, while many South Africans are beating each other on the shoulder about the non-existent changes that have taken place in South Africa.

They have an almost maniacal hatred for anybody who asks just what has changed in South Africa today?[25]

Meanwhile, faced with increased guerilla activity as well as increased mass activity, the regime continues preparing on every front for intensified efforts to try to save apartheid from the forces of resistance and liberation.

References

Abbreviations
DD   *Daily Dispatch,* East London
CT   *Cape Times,* Cape Town
Debates House of Assembly and Senate
        Debates, Cape Town
FM   *Financial Mail,* Johannesburg
GN   *Guardian,* London
NW   *Natal Witness,* Durban
Post   *Post,* Johannesburg

RDM   *Rand Daily Mail,* Johannesburg
RDMX *Rand Daily Mail Extra,* Johannes-
        burg (township edition)
Star   *Star* weekly airmail edition,
        Johannesburg
SE   *Sunday Express,* Johannesburg
SP   *Sunday Post,* Johannesburg
Times   *Times,* London
FOCUS *Focus on Political Repression* (IDAF)

INTRODUCTION

1. *Star* 8.2.78
2. *RDMX* 31.12.76.
3. *GN* 22.9.79.
4. see Barbara Rogers, *Divide and Rule* (IDAF, 1976)
5. *Post* 7.4.78.
6. *FM* 16.11.78.
7. Dr. H. F. Verwoerd, Minister of Native Affairs, introducing Bantu Education Bill, *Senate Debates* 7.6.54.
8. *RDMX* 11.3.79.
9. *RDMX* 11.1.78.
10. *RDMX* 26.7.78.
11. SA Institute of Race Relations *Survey 1978* (Johannesburg, 1979) p. 161.
12. *FM* 16.2.79.
13. *RDMX* 10.1.78.
14. *RDMX* 14.9.78.
15. H. Santa Cruz, *Racial Discrimination* (United Nations, 1976) quoting from *Assembly Debates* 1963.
16. *Land Tenure Conditions in South Africa* (UN Centre against Apartheid. Notes and Documents No. 37/76, December 1976) p. 64.
17. see SAIRR *Survey 1978,* p. 562.
18. *SP* 1.4.79.
19. *RDM* 21.12.78.
20. *FM* 16.11.78.
21. *FM* 9.11.79.
22. *FM* 1.12.78.
23. *GN* 22.11.78.
24. *Times* 21.12.79.
25. Harry Oppenheimer, 5th Stock Exchange Chairman's Lecture, London, 18.5.76.
26. Ruth First et al., *The South African Connection* (London, 1973) p. 30.
27. (Riekert) Commission of Inquiry into Legislation Affecting the Utilisation of Manpower, *Report* (Pretoria, 1979) Table 3.2.
28. see n. 25 above.

Part One: CONCESSIONS?

THE TOWNSHIPS

1. *FM* 1.2.80.
2. quoted in Riekert *Report,* para. 4.393.
3. SAIRR *Survey 1977,* p. 381.
4. *ibid,* p. 382.
5. Native Representative Council *Proceedings 1946,* (Pretoria, 1946) pp. 36-41.
6. *Post* 12.1.78.
7. *Post* 6.5.79.
8. *RDMX* 20.2.79.
9. *Post* 30.4.78.
10. *RDM* 18.9.79.
11. *RDMX* 17.4.78.
12. *RDMX* 26.9.79.
13. *RDM* 25.9.78.
14. *Post* 29.9.78.
15. *Post* 28.9.79.
16. Deputy Minister of Co-operation and Development, quoted in *RDM* 7.9.79.
17. SAIRR *Survey 1978,* p. 335.
18. *RDM* 10.8.79.
19. *RDM* 7.9.79. Dr. Koornhof has denied that he said this in so many words. The RDM insists the content of his speech justified the report, and it is notable that Dr. Koornhof has not tried prosecuting the RDM over this under South Africa's press laws.
20. *FM* 6.7.79.
21. *ibid.*
22. *CT* 27.7.79.
23. *RDMX* 27.8.76.
24. *Star* 4.11.77.
25. *RDMX* 7.1.78.
26. *Post* 3.5.78.
27. *Post* 20.9.78.
28. *SP* 17.12.78.
29. *ibid.*
30. *RDMX* 2.3.79.
31. *Post* 1.4.79.
32. *Star* 20.4.79.
33. *ibid.*
34. *SP* 1.7.79.
35. *Post* 19.10.79.
36. *FM* 19.10.79.
37. SAIRR *Survey 1978* p. 337.
38. Black Sash, *Emergency Report,* November 1979.
39. *RDMX* 18.11.77.
40. *RDMX* 14.9.78.

41. *RDMX* 30.3.79.
42. *RDM* 8.8.79.
43. *RDMX* 21.3.79.
44. *NW* 28.9.79.
45. *RDM* 5.11.79.
46. *Post* 27.7.79.
47. *RDM* 13.10.79.
48. *RDMX* 13.11.78.
49. *Star* 22.2.79.
50. *Star* 1.2.79.
51. *Post* 22.1.79.
52. *Post* 25.1.79.
53. *Post* 30.1.79.
54. *Post* 8.3.79.
55. *RDMX/Post* 7.3.79.
56. *RDMX* 16.12.78.

RACE SEPARATION

1. *SE* 25.3.79.
2. Centre for Intergroup Studies, Cape Town, *Facilities* (Draft No. 8, December 1978) p. 14.
3. *RDM* 1.8.79.
4. *CT* 21.7.78.
5. *Star* 9.1.80.
6. *GN* 2.9.79.
7. Centre for Intergroup Studies, Draft No. 8, *op cit.*
8. *GN* 11.12.79.
9. *RDM* 15.8.79.
10. *GN* 25.7.79; *RDM* 1.8.79.
11. *Star* 30.12.78.
12. *RDM* 28.12.79.
13. *GN* 27.9.79.
14. SAIRR *Survey 1977*, p. 53.
15. *GN* 27.9.79.
16. *RDM* 26.10.79.
17. *RDM* 23.10.79.
18. *GN* 7.2.80.
19. SAIRR *Survey 1977*, p. 588. For an account of discrimination in sport and the attempts to introduce 'multi-national' sporting events see Joan Brickhill, *Race Against Race: South Africa's "Multi-national" Sport Fraud* (IDAF, 1976).
20. SAIRR *Survey 1977*, p. 588.
21. *ibid*, p. 559.
22. *ST* 7.5.78.
23. *ST* 30.4.76; *Argus* (Cape Town) 20.5.76.
24. *SA Digest* (Pretoria) 4.11.78.
25. SAIRR *Survey 1978*, p. 496.
26. *GN* 8.9.79.
27. SAIRR *Survey 1978*, p. 489.
28. *ibid*, p. 339.
29. *Debates* 28.2.79; 14.3.79.

POLITICAL POWER

1. *Post* 13.5.79.
2. *Post* 30.1.79.
3. *Post* 13.7.79.
4. *Post* 19.7.79.
5. *RDM* 7/8.4.76.
6. SAIRR *Survey 1977*, p. 9.
7. The provisions of the constitutional proposals are outlined in SAIRR *Survey 1977* pp. 7-10 and *Survey 1979* pp. 4-5. The Constitutional Draft Bill was published in the *Government Gazette* 3.4.79.
8. Draft Bill, p. 52.
9. *GN* 12.11.79.

THE ECONOMIC SPHERE

1. *FM* 17.2.78.
2. *RDMX* 28.9.78.
3. *GN* 3.11.79.
4. *Sunday Times* (London) 25.11.79.
5. *FM* 16.11.79.
6. Dr. Simon Brand, quoted in *RDM* 5.11.79.
7. (Wiehahn) Commission of Inquiry into Labour Legislation, *Report* (Pretoria, 1979) para. 1.2.
8. *ibid*, para. 1.4.
9. *RDM* 30.10.79.
10. Wiehahn *Report*, para. 3.35.5.
11. *ibid*, 3.35.5.
12. *ibid*, 3.58.2.
13. *ibid*, 3.58.1.
14. *ibid*, 3.58.3.
15. *ibid*, 3.58.1.
16. *ibid*, 3.35.1.
17. *ibid*, 1.10.
18. *ibid*, 3.35.7.
19. *ibid*, 3.8.
20. *ibid*, 3.20.6.
21. *ibid*, 3.20.4.
22. *ibid*, 3.71.
23. *ibid*, 3.129.
24. *FM* 21.9.79.
25. *South African Journal of Labour Relations*, Sept. 1979, p. 19.
26. *ibid*.
27. BBC Interview 3.10.79.
28. *SP* 8.7.79.
29. *RDM* 26.9.79.
30. *FM* 28.9.79.
31. *NW* 6.11.79.
32. *FT* 5.11.79.
33. *FM* 28.9.79.
34. *ibid*.
35. National Party leaflet distributed during June 1979 in Randfontein constituency, reprinted in *South African Labour Bulletin*
36. *FM* 25.1.80.
37. *ibid*.

Part Two: REPRESSION

1. Black Sash Emergency Report, November 1979.
2. *FM* 28.9.79.
3. *SP* 2.9.79.

RESIDENCE

4. *RDMX* 1.4.78.
5. *RDMX* 15.4.78.
6. *Debates* 3.5.78.
7. *RDMX* 14.6.78.
8. *RDMX* 5.3.79.
9. *Post* 14.2.79.
10. *SE* 6.4.79.
11. *RDM* 4.3.80.
12. *RDMX* 7.9.78.

13. *RDMX* 14.9.78.
14. *RDMX* 18.9.78.
15. *ST* 17.9.78.
16. *Star* 2.10.78.
17. *SP* 22.7.79.
18. *RDMX* 6.4.79.
19. SAIRR *Survey 1978*, p. 352.
20. *RDM* 28.9.79.
21. *GN* 10.12.79.
22. Crossroads Action Committee leaflet n.d.
23. *SP* 26.11.78.
24. *Post* 3/20.12.78.
25. *Post* 20.12.78.
26. Crossroads Action Committee leaflet; *SP* 3.6.79.
27. *DD* 26.10.79.
28. *Star* 5.10.78.
29. *Post* 6.10.78.
30. *RDMX* 2.12.78.
31. *Debates* 21.3.79.
32. *NW* 19.5.79.
33. *SP* 2.9.79.
34. *Post* 19.2.79.
35. *Post* 26.7.79.
36. *SP* 29.7.79; 16.10.79.
37. *RDM* 4.3.79.
38. *ibid*.
39. *RDMX* 22/23/29.8.78.
40. *RDMX* 14.9.78.
41. *Post* 12.9.78.
42. *Sunday Times* (London) 25.11.79.
43. BBC *Survey of World Broadcasts* 13.6.79
44. *Post* 25.1.78.
45. *SP* 21.1.79.
46. *Post* 21.1.79.
47. SAIRR *Survey 1978*, p. 174.
48. *ibid*.
49. *ibid*, p. 175.
50. Riekert *Report*, para. 4.234.

THE URBAN ORDER

1. Riekert *Report*, para. 1.8.
2. *ibid*, para. 3.70.
3. *ibid*, para. 4.152.
4. *ibid*, para. 6.14 (u).
5. *ibid*, para. 3.157.
6. *ibid*, para. 4.210.
7. SAIRR *Survey 1978*, pp. 176-7.
8. Riekert *Report*, para. 4.53.
9. *ibid*, para. 4.47.
10. *ibid*, para. 4.152.
11. White Paper WP/T/1979 p. 3.
12. Riekert *Report*, para. 4.157.
13. *ibid*, para. 4.185.
14. *ibid*.
15. *ibid*, para. 4.204.
16. *ibid*, para. 4.210.
17. quoted in *FM* 6.7.79.
18. Riekert *Report*, para. 4.206.
19. *ibid*, para. 4.208.
20. White Paper WP/T p. 10.
21. Riekert *Report*, para. 3.216.
22. *ibid*, para. 4.277.
23. White Paper WP/T, pp. 5, 9.
24. *RDM* 16.2.80.
25. White Paper, p. 10.
26. *RDM* 14.7.79.
27. *RDM* 1/10.8.79.
28. *FM* 20.7.79.

29. Black Sash Emergency Report, *op cit*.
30. *RDM* 19.9.79.
31. *Post* 19.7.79.
32. *Post* 22.8.79.
33. *Post* 29.8.79.
34 *Post* 29.9.79.
35. *Post* 26.7.79.
36. SAIRR *Survey 1978*, p. 335.
37. *CT* 4.7.79; 28.8.79.
38. *Post* 16.7.79.
39. *Post* 19.7.79.
40. Black Sash Emergency Report, *op. cit*.

SECURITY

1. SAIRR *Survey 1978*, p. 67.
2. *Government Gazette* No. 6576, 13.7.79.
3. *Debates* 26.5.79.
4. See *RDM*, *Post*, Star 11/13.9.78.
5. SAIRR *Survey 1978*, p. 41.
6. *Post* 28.9.79.
7. *GN* 24.12.79.
8. SAIRR *Survey 1978*, p. 76.
9. *ibid*, p. 117.
10. *FOCUS on Political Repression* (IDAF) No. 24 p. 5.
11. *Post* 9.4.79.
12. *FOCUS*, No. 22 p. 7.
13. *SE* 11.3.77.
14. *SE* 18.3.79.
15. *Star* 16.6.78.
16. *Post* 13.3.79.
17. SAIRR *Survey 1978*, p. 40.
18. see FOCUS No. 29.

CONCEALMENT

1. White Paper WP/T, op. cit., p. 11.
2. Dept. of Education and Training, *Annual Report 1972* p. 2.
3. *Post* 9.2.79.
4. *SP* 11.2.79.
5. *SE* 8.7.79.
6. *Voice* 7.7.79.
7. Black Sash Emergency Report, *op. cit*.
8. *ibid*.
9. *Post* 7.9.79.
10. *GN* 10.11.79.
11. quoted in *Inquiry* (Rhodes University, Grahamstown) 1979 p. 12.
12. *ibid*.
13. *ibid*.
14. *RDMX* 5.5.79.
15. *Post* 19.4.79.
16. *Inquiry*, p. 18.
17. *RDMX* 5.5.79.
18. *Inquiry* p. 18.
19. *RDMX* 5.5.79.
20. *Eastern Province Herald* (Port Elizabeth) 13.4.79.
21. *RDM* 17.8.79.
22. *SP* 8.4.79.

CONCLUSION

1. Speech to Foreign Policy Association, New York, 18.12.79. (FCO, London).
2. *Star* 29.8.79.
3. *CT* 23.11.79.
4. *CT* 19.3.79.
5. *FM* 9.11.79.
6. *FM* 16.11.79.

7. *Star* 9.4.79.
8. *Star* 9.4.79; *RDM* 10.4.79.
9. *Post* 29.8.79; 29.9.79.
10. *RDM* 13.10.79.
11. *RDM* 13.10.79.
12. *DN* 12.9.79.
13. *NW* 28.9.79.
14. *Post* 19.9.79.
15. *CT* 2/3.10.79; *RDM* 10.10.79.
16. *DN* 26.10.79.
17. *RDM* 2.11.79.
18. *GN* 5.1.80.
19. *CT* 3.11.79; the black union, the UAW, was also caught in a dilemma by the strike. Because it was a "political" issue instead of a work issue, the union felt they should not take it up, a decision which led to hostility to the union within the workforce. (Under the Wiehahn recommendations, legal unions may not take up political issues.)
20. *FM* 23.11.79.
21. *CT* 24.11.79.
22. *CT* 21/22.11.79; *RDM* 23.11.79.
23. *CT* 11.12.79; *RDM* 7.12.79.
24. *RDM* 21.11.79.
25. *GN* 12.1.80.
26. *ibid.*
27. *GN* 16.10.79.
28. *Times* 12.8.78.
29. *Star* 20.3.79.
30. *RDMX* 5.12.78.
31. *GN* 22.9.79.
32. *GN* 3.11.79.
33. *ibid.*
34. *Star* 5.4.79.
35. *Post* 7.9.79.
36. *GN* 12.11.79.

POSTSCRIPT

1. *Times* 1.7.80.
2. *Times* 1.9.80. See also 1975 and 1977 White Papers on Defence.
3. *DD* 30.4.80.
4. "The Great Evasion: South Africa. A Survey", *Economist* 21.6.80.
5. *Post* 17.7.80.
6. *RDM* 19.8.80.
7. *FM* 11.1.80.
8. *FOCUS* No. 30.
9. *RDM* 31.7.80.
10. *RDM* 1.8.80.
11. *GN* 19.9.80.
12. *FOCUS* Nos. 29-31.
13. *CT* 9.5.80; *RDM* 9.5.80, 30.5.80.
14. *Sunday Times* Johannesburg 28.9.80.
15. *CT* 31.7.80.
16. *GN* 11.8.80.
17. *DD* 30.4.80.
18. *GN* 24.6.80.
19. *Star* 9.8.80.
20. *CT* 2.9.80.
21. *SE* 27.7.80.
22. *Star* 13.9.80.
23. *Times* 1.7.80.
24. *SE* 3.8.80.
25. *Post* 24.7.80.
26. *Times* 24.2.80, 22.8.80, 1.9.80; *RDM* 23.4.80, 13.6.80.

Printed by A. G. Bishop & Sons Ltd., Orpington, Kent